Arnold Tompkins

The Philosophy of Teaching

Arnold Tompkins

The Philosophy of Teaching

ISBN/EAN: 9783337003845

Printed in Europe, USA, Canada, Australia, Japan

Cover: Foto ©Paul-Georg Meister /pixelio.de

More available books at **www.hansebooks.com**

THE
PHILOSOPHY OF TEACHING

BY

ARNOLD TOMPKINS

AUTHOR OF "THE SCIENCE OF DISCOURSE"

"*I would not creep along the coast, but steer
Out in mid-sea, by guidance of the stars*"

BOSTON, U.S.A.
GINN & COMPANY, PUBLISHERS
1899

COPYRIGHT, 1891 AND 1894
BY
ARNOLD TOMPKINS

ALL RIGHTS RESERVED

CONTENTS.

	PAGE
INTRODUCTION	vii–xii
THE TEACHING PROCESS	1–35
Its Nature and Elements	1
Illustration of the Process	11
Gain in Lesson Planning	29
AIM IN TEACHING	36–72
Diversity of Aims	36
Aim found in Nature of Life	42
As an Inner Process	42
As an Outer Process	55
Unification of Aims	63
METHOD IN TEACHING	73–275
The Universal Law	73
The Two Organic Phases of the Process	75
The Two Factors in the Process	79
The Ultimate Ground of Unity	93
The Ultimate Law of Unity	97
Specific Phases of the Law	109
Thinking the Individual	115
1. As Fixed or Coexistent. — Description	119

CONTENTS.

	PAGE
(a) By Means of Attributes	120
(b) By Means of Parts	138
(c) By Means of Another Individual	143
2. As Changing, or Successive. — Narration	145
(a) By Means of Attributes	147
(b) By Means of Parts	149
(c) By Means of Another Individual	151
3. Applications of the Foregoing: (a) In Geography; (b) in Physiology; (c) in History; (d) in Composition; (e) in Reading	153
Thinking the General	183
1. Forming the General Notion. — Exposition	185
(a) Thinking the Content of a Class	187
(1) Steps and Laws	188
(2) Educational Value	192
(b) Thinking the Extent of a Class	194
(1) Steps and Laws	195
(2) Educational Value	197
(c) The Processes Moving in Unity	198
(d) Exposition of Ideal Truth	203
2. Applying the General Notion. — Argumentation	214
(a) The Processes in an Argument	220
(1) Controlled by Relation of Extent	220
(a) Deduction	220
(b) Induction	225
(c) Identification	230
(2) Controlled by the Relation of Cause and Effect	231
(a) *A Priori* Arguments	235
(b) *A Posteriori* Arguments	240

	PAGE
THE PROCESS AS A COMPLEX WHOLE	246
The Objective Factor	247
The Subjective Factor	251
Problems Solved by the Law	260
1. Concentration	261
2. Enriching the Course of Study	261
3. Correlation of Studies	263
4. Educational Values	265
5. Morals in the Public School	267
6. Religion in the Public School	270

NOTE. — As this book first appeared it contained a concluding chapter on "School Management," which is now omitted with the hope of giving that phase of pedagogics more adequate treatment in a separate volume. This volume is strictly confined to the essential nature and laws of the teaching process; reserving for separate treatment the organized means in making the teaching process effective. This organized means — the school — is grounded in, and arises out of, the nature and laws of the teaching process; hence "School Management" is the logical sequence of the present treatment; and should be rounded out, as the other hemisphere of the teacher's life, from the same central point of view.

ARNOLD TOMPKINS.

CHICAGO, ILL., May 10, 1894.

INTRODUCTION.

The term "philosophy of teaching" places the accent on the process of teaching, while the term "philosophy of education" emphasizes the system of principles as such. The philosophy of education will not be attempted; the theme being restricted to the application of philosophic principles to the teaching process. Not that the application of principles is a more worthy object of attention than the system of principles themselves, but because I feel moved to show how helpful in practice, daily and hourly, are the universal principles which philosophy announces.

I have no sympathy with the sneer at mere theorists — those who seek principles for their own sake. What should we do without the light they throw upon our pathway! The practical teacher is not always conscious of, and thankful for, the great service rendered by the speculative philosopher. Universal truth seems so remote from the immediate, concrete details of school work that we do not suspect its presence and controlling power. Hegel well protests against the thought that philosophy deals with another world; asserting its subject to be the concrete and ever present facts of life. The practical teacher must sooner or later learn that inspiration and guidance through the daily routine of duty must be sought in universal truth; that specific rules and recipes, which seem to be so helpful because of their easy and immediate application, are really impractical and confusing because they have no germinant power and breadth of application; that his bearings must be taken from the fixed stars, and not from the shifting scenes and lights of the lower atmosphere.

The application of universal principles to teaching presupposes a philosophy of education; and the existence of such a philosophy is not always admitted. Even that there is a science of education has been denied; and for stronger reasons may its philosophy be questioned, it being a higher generalization of principles. A distinguished writer, in the *Educational Review*, discusses at length the question, "Is there a science of education?" and concludes in these words: "To sum all up in a word, teaching is an art. Therefore there is indeed no science of education."

That there is not yet a fairly well organized and complete system of educational principles may be readily admitted. But the impossibility of such a science is affirmed on the ground that teaching is an art. This conclusion, however, taken apart from the reasoning on which it is based, does not represent the writer fairly. The drift of the article shows him to mean this: There is no science whose generalizations will fit the concrete case in every act of teaching; that there are special conditions and individual peculiarities that no principle can anticipate. But there is no science of any kind whose generalizations exactly fit the concrete case. The individuals brought into scientific system retain their individuality. We doubt not that there is a science of vertebrates; or think the science of them the less perfect or the less valuable because each vertebrate has countless characteristics which the generalizations must ignore. In fact, it would not be a science without such differences. In order to have a science, the general fact, or law, must be seen as manifesting itself in diversity of individuals. Generalizations of science are not abstractions; but, to be generalizations, must retain their hold on the individuals.

While no other teaching act is just like the one in which that individual teacher instructs that individual pupil, yet that act has essential marks and common elements with every other teaching act. It is the divine skill of the born teacher's instinct that seizes the peculiarity, which seems to annul the law; yet the law is there, and must also be discerned, or the peculiarity could not be known as such. The tact and personal insight of the teacher required in every act of teaching is not to be guided by the immediate consciousness of general principles; but this does not prove that there is no science of teaching, or that such a science is not of supreme value, even to the divinely gifted teacher.

If, in order to be a science, generalizations must be made which shall blot out all peculiarities of each teaching act, so that the teacher needs to apply only monotonous rules, which require no personal insight into the peculiarities of the immediate case, then indeed there is no science of teaching possible; then not even desirable. The science of teaching must leave room for the individual element; as does, without question, any other science. It must ever be remembered that the individual case is not wholly peculiar; that the most essential thing in it is that which is found in every other case. The peculiarity may be so prominent as to thrust the universal element into the background; but the universal element gives law to the act of teaching. The science of education brings diversity under law. It must enable the teacher to bring into consciousness the essential elements of all teaching in every particular act of it.

The philosophy of teaching, as distinguished from the science, gives distinct emphasis to the universal element, showing its controlling power in all that the teacher does. It is the explanation of the teaching process by means of universal law. By it the separate acts are brought, not only into unity among themselves, which constitutes merely the science of teaching, but they are brought into the unity of the complete system of means of spiritual growth. Science explains a group of phenomena by a principle, or law, oc- extensive with the group explained. At least, emphasis is given to such a principle. Philosophy explains a group of phenomena by some principle, or law, which extends beyond the group explained to all other groups. The science of grammar brings all sentences into their own unity; that is, into unity among themselves; while the philosophy of grammar brings the unity established by science into the unity of the universe. It is this larger unity alone which illumines the whole pathway of the teacher, and yields assured guidance to the goal of his labor.

Dignity of work does not depend on what one does, but on being consciously controlled, in the doing, by universal law. The teacher who is conscious only of the individual process before him, is on the lowest possible plane of unskilled labor; he is the slave of recipes and devices. As by degrees he comes under the controlling power of higher and still higher generality of law, he rises from the automatic action of a mere operative to the plane of rational insight and self-direction. The highest plane is that in which universal law guides the hand and inspires the heart. The whole sky of truth bends over each recitation; and the teacher needs but climb Sinai to receive the divine law. All the laws of thought and being pervade the teaching process; all philosophy is back of it. At first, Aristotle, Kant, Hegel, and Spencer seem remote from the immediate work of the teacher. This remoteness must be made to disappear; the ends of the earth must be brought together; the universal laws of spiritual life must become native atmosphere to the teacher. We harm ourselves and degrade our work in holding philosophy to be of another world; that the philosophy of education is one thing, and the practice of educating another thing; that the philosophy of education belongs to the professional philosophizer on great educational problems, rather than to the day-laborer in the vineyard. It is said that philosophy can bake no bread, but that she can secure to us God and immortality. This ought to be sufficient. But she can bake bread, and must do so or miss God and immortality. To secure heaven she must mix with the daily affairs of earth ; and while searching out God and immortality, must bring counsel and comfort to the day-laborer in the school-room.

THE TEACHING PROCESS.

ITS NATURE AND ELEMENTS.

As a basis for discussing the higher unity of the teaching process, let us bring before the mind the lower unity of the process; the common nature of teaching acts among themselves considered — the science of teaching recalled as the basis for the philosophy of teaching.

General Nature. — 1. Teaching is a process, because it is a series of steps to the realization of an end; which end is the motive in the series — the beginning of the series. The end, as idea, moves forward to realize itself. This requires means in producing the steps. Thus we have in a process the end, or purpose, to be realized; the steps which lie between the end as idea and the end as objective reality; and the means by which the steps are taken. Every teaching process has these organic elements in common with every other process.

2. Teaching is a mental process; not a mechanical one. This ought to go without saying; but there is a general feeling that teaching is the manipulation of mechanical means. This feeling is manifested in the current phrases used in speaking of method; as, the topical method, the outline method, the diagram method, the laboratory

method, the library method, the lecture method, etc. Teaching is not the manipulation of external means; as, tapping the bell, calling the roll, making records and reports, correcting the wayward, applying forms of drill to put knowledge into the mind and fasten it there, and the like. Every teaching act, and school work in general, has its mechanical phase; but this is not its essential, its vital, one. It is easy to become lost in the formal process; for it is ever present, and is the obtrusive element. The first view of school work is that of a formal external process; and it requires reflection to penetrate through the letter which "killeth" to the spirit which "maketh alive."

The consciousness of manipulating machinery instead of conducting a spiritual process, an experience of growth on the part of the learner, is the main root of all school errors, and has its origin in the belief that knowing itself is a mechanical process,— a belief that the mind is a receptacle, called memory, to hold what is put into it; and that learning is receiving and retaining something foreign to the self. The mind being a receptacle, the teacher is, by means of contrivance of lever, wheel, and rope, to transfer some ponderable, external stuff into it. The machinery by which this is done becomes the important factor, and the manipulation of it the chief process involved; for knowing, as usually conceived, is not a process, and the mind is something other than that which it knows.

It is a long step toward freedom when the teacher awakens to the fact that teaching is a spiritual process below the form; that it is the vital touch of the teacher's mind with the mind in which the knowledge is born, and not that of external relation of transferring something to it manufactured elsewhere than in the mind learning. The wind may bear the fecundating pollen to the stigma; but the process of flowering and fruiting is another matter. Some phase of the bondage to the formal and mechanical has been the object of attack of all educational reformers; and must continue to receive their attention, for each generation falls into the bondage anew. Every teacher, in learning his art, must strive earnestly from the first to live in consciousness of the spiritual movement below the form; and to hold the form as the mere varying surface play of that movement.

3. It has been said that teaching is a mental process, in which the mind of the teacher comes in vital touch with the mind of the learner. The mind of the teacher moves forward in the same line of thought, feeling, and volition with the mind of the one taught. The teacher cannot produce in the learner a given experience without having first produced in himself that experience. If the teacher is to cause the pupil to think the position, form, size, cause, and effects of the Gulf Stream, the teacher himself must think each of these relations while stimulating the pupil to think each of them. If patriotism is to be aroused by teaching "Barbara Frietchie," the teacher himself must be stirred by that feeling while causing the pupil to experience it. Thus the two minds are always one in the mental steps required to learn an object; and, also, in the emotion

to be cultivated and the resolution to be strengthened. The teacher passes into some act or state of experience, and the pupil rises, at the touch of the teacher, into the same experience.

An important inference from the foregoing should be noted. It is an old saying that as the teacher so the school. The best meaning for this is, that the pupil's mind, in the act of learning, becomes like the teacher's mind; it takes on the tone and coloring of the teacher's thought. The teacher builds his own thought structure into the mind of the pupil; begets in him his own purity, strength, and sweep of emotional life; breathes into him the breath of his own ethical nature. The teacher may resolve to train to accurate, thorough, and methodical habits of thought; but unless these are habits of his own mind his efforts will be unavailing. The stream cannot rise higher than its source. If the teacher thinks loosely and slovenly he cannot hope to realize anything better in the pupil, so far as the teaching goes. The narrow pedant and dogmatist can never secure scholarly habits and liberal culture. The teacher who has not a rich and full range of emotional life can expect nothing but a withered soul born of his teaching. The man who has not strength and purity of character cannot strengthen and purify character. The teacher builds his life into that of his pupil; and it is absolutely essential that his life be all that he expects his pupil to become. The quality of a teacher's life is a part of his professional equipment.

Particular Nature. — 1. While the teacher's mind and that of the pupil take the same steps in the process of teaching and of learning, there must be the essential difference which makes the one teaching and the other learning. The difference lies here : while the pupil thinks the object under consideration, the teacher thinks the pupil's process of thinking the object. For example, there are a certain number of fixed mental steps necessary on the part of the pupil to gain the idea adjective : (1) he perceives, (2) imagines, (3) compares and contrasts, (4) reasons, and (5) generalizes. The pupil must move through these forms of activity, but he is not conscious of the movement. His whole conscious effort is expended on the object studied. He says, I find this and this and this in the object; not that now I am perceiving, imagining, etc. The teacher must be conscious of the process of the pupil in knowing the object in the act of producing that process ; for how else could he rationally produce it? The difference is between thinking the object and thinking the process of thinking the object. The pupil, in the study of geography, is thinking the earth ; but in teaching geography the teacher must think the pupil's thinking of the earth. It follows that the steps of the teacher, which are identical with those of the pupil, as before explained, must be represented steps ; the knowledge must be old knowledge. The teacher has before taken the steps in knowing the adjective ; so that in teaching he is relieved from any conscious effort in learning it, and may put his whole attention to the pupil's process of learning it. This suggests the necessity for the teacher's familiarity with the subject-matter of instruction.

One phase of a teacher's professional knowledge of a subject is obvious from the foregoing. An academic knowledge of grammar enables the student to think the subject of grammar; while the teacher's knowledge of that subject enables him to think grammar into the processes of the learning mind. As a basis for this the teacher must know the subject of grammar and the mind learning it; but the professional aspect of the work appears when the teacher resolves grammar into the mental processes of the pupil; or, brings the pupil's processes into the form of grammar. All professional treatment of subject-matter resolves it into the mental experience of the learner.

2. While the pupil and the teacher take the steps necessary in learning the object, the series of steps taken by the teacher bear the relation of cause to those taken by the pupil; and without external means the teacher cannot reproduce his experience in the pupil. There must be questions, directions, illustrations, etc., to stimulate the pupil's mind to take the step designed by the teacher. If the pupil is to infer the cause of the climate in a given locality, the means must be adjusted to that mental act. The teacher first thinks the steps to be taken in the pupil's thought, and then he adjusts the external means to each step. Skill in giving directions and in asking questions arises out of the readiness with which the teacher, by insight and sympathy, finds his way into the mind of the

pupil in his effort to learn. Books on questioning avail little; it is the quick and true insight of the teacher into the essential movement of the learner's mind that enables him to hit on the right turn of question or neat adjustment of device. Now, the pupil does not hold the relation of this external means to his internal experience; but this the teacher must do. While thinking one of the pupil's steps he must think, also, the means by which he may cause the pupil to take that step.

3. Thus far, teaching appears to be the conscious act of producing mental experience in the pupil; and that there is in the process two conscious elements, making the act complex: consciousness of the experience in the act of producing it, and consciousness of the means by which to produce it. The third, and last, factor of which the teacher is conscious is that of the effect of the experience produced on the character of the pupil. In fact, the experience is produced because a certain end in life is to be reached. The rational teacher says to himself that the pupil's spiritual growth requires a given course of experience, and then he proceeds to adjust means to secure that experience. It is impossible to conceive how one can conduct a process without being conscious of the aim in the process. All the steps must be brought into the unity of the aim. If to-day the teacher is to cause the pupil to think Westminster Abbey and to arouse certain emotions by that object, he should be able to state how the knowledge, and how such thinking and feeling, helps the child to realize the aim of life. In planning a lesson it is not enough to say that the

purpose is to give a knowledge of the object under consideration and to cultivate certain faculties; but it must be made clear how such knowledge, with the activities involved, is for the ultimate spiritual good of the pupil. The teacher's question always is, How can I wield this subject-matter to make it educative? or better, What subject-matter will administer unto the child's spiritual necessities, and how can it be wielded to make it bear its full effect in the mind taught? Every lesson requires the teacher to hold in mind the entire compass of the pupil's life; and seeing what must be the outcome of the whole, he brings the bit of experience into unity with the life movement as a whole.

If the doctrine be true that man's highest happiness comes from consciousness of realizing ideals, it is obvious that the teacher can find no true pleasure in his work without the consciousness of realizing some end set up in the life of the pupil. That teacher is happiest who feels that, in the process of teaching, the highest good in life is being realized by the one taught. The teacher who seeks true pleasure in his work, and hopes to find the reward of his labor in the thing done, and who expects to thrill the pupil with the joy of spiritual activity and growth, must find the secret in the consciousness of realizing the highest good of life; in ministering unto the deepest cravings of the soul for truth, beauty, and virtue.

It thus appears that teaching is a conscious process having three organic elements: (1) consciousness of the mental experience in the act of producing it, (2) of the means of stimulating the experience in the pupil, and (3) of the value, or purpose, of the experience in the unfolding life of the pupil. Put in the form of a definition: *Teaching is the conscious process of producing mental experience for the purpose of life development;* or, to rid this of its tautology, *Teaching is the process by which one mind, from set purpose, produces the life-unfolding process in another.*

The subjective process above described is not teaching till its counterpart is realized in the objective process of the recitation. The triple idea in the mind of the teacher realizes itself in the external process with the pupil, having the three elements corresponding with those in the subjective process. The elements, however, are reversed as the process held in the mind of the teacher realizes itself in the class taught.

In observing a recitation, the thing noted first in order of time, and first as logical condition, is the external means employed by the teacher; such as directions, questions, statements, illustrations, etc. The second element in time, and in logical relation, is the experience produced; and the last is the good resulting to the learner. But the process in the mind of the teacher has a reverse order. The good of the child must be first in mind; then, and not before, the experience necessary to that good may be considered; and the experience to be produced necessarily precedes in thought the stimulus to that experience.

True, in practice we do not always follow this logical order of thought; but rather begin with the subject-matter to be taught, feeling that it is reading, writing, etc., that we teach, instead of the child. One of the most striking features of Froebel's great work was that of beginning with the child; and, having ascertained its needs, he proceeded to the course of mental activity essential to its needs; and then he invented a system of means, the kindergarten gifts, by which the educative activity could be produced. Had he contributed nothing to educational thought and practice but this order of procedure, he would be properly called an educational reformer. A great reform will have been made when we take our bearings from the standpoint of the child, and not from arithmetic, geography, etc., as mere subject-matter; as something external to the life of the pupil and to be taught for its own sake.

This reversal of the subjective order of thought in the mind of the teacher, as it becomes realized in the external act of the recitation, is shown more clearly by this outline:—

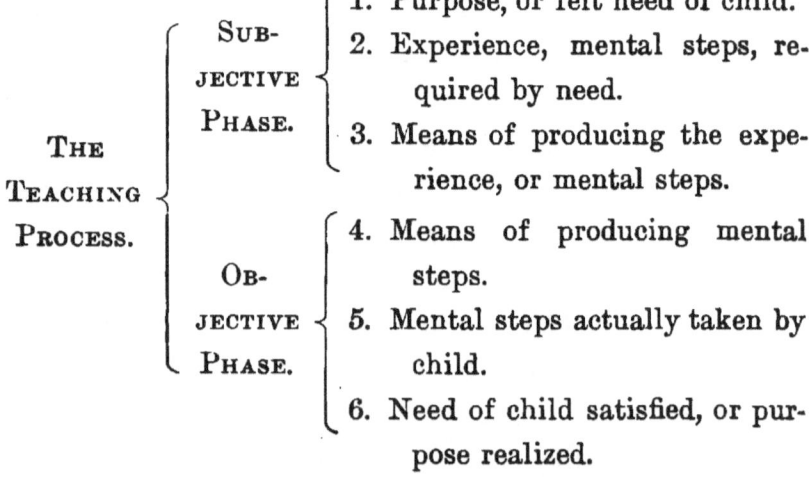

The Teaching Process.
- Subjective Phase.
  1. Purpose, or felt need of child.
  2. Experience, mental steps, required by need.
  3. Means of producing the experience, or mental steps.
- Objective Phase.
  4. Means of producing mental steps.
  5. Mental steps actually taken by child.
  6. Need of child satisfied, or purpose realized.

The process folds back upon itself; it is a series which returns unto itself, as in any other organic process. The first is last and the last is first. The two phases are not separate in time, but exist at the same moment — move parallel, the subjective as the constant and immediate cause of the objective.

But when one is asked to prepare a lesson on a bit of given subject-matter, as the noun, a river, a battle, he must begin with the second element in the process; because the subject-matter is supposed to have been already determined upon in the light of some educational end. In this case the teacher is first to make out the round of mental activity which the given point to be taught is capable of producing. With this as a basis, he can state both the educational value of the activity produced and the means of producing the activity; and either of these may be stated first, since both are directly based on the object to be taught, regarded as a mental process. First, then, in the practical work of planning a lesson the teacher will analyze the object to be taught into the mental processes which constitute it; and then proceed to deduce from that process both the educative power and the means of wielding the process to make it bear its full value to the learner. This order will, therefore, be followed in the —

Illustration of the Process.

Suppose the idea pyramid is to be taught to a primary class, say a third-reader grade. This being given as the starting point, the first step in planning the lesson is that of analyzing the idea into the mental movement which constitutes it.

The Movement — *As a whole.* — The mind must form this new idea out of the elements of old knowledge. Let it be supposed that the knowledge most immediately connected with the new idea are the ideas solid, flat surface, straight line, triangle, and point. Then the movement as a whole is a movement from these ideas to the idea pyramid. In planning any lesson the teacher must state the point from which and the point to which the mind moves — bound the movement as a whole. But this is not all; the general character of the movement as a whole must be noted. The act as a whole is an act of synthesis; the pupil synthesizes the known elements into the unity of the pyramid.

While there is a fixed relation of the elements constituting the pyramid, each individual pyramid which the mind may create or observe must have its essential elements more or less obscured by individual peculiarities. The pupil is to think the diversity as shown by individual pyramids into the unity of the single idea pyramid, — a movement from the diversity of individuals to the unity of a concept.

Steps in the movement. — The movement towards unity must be made along all the threads which bind the individuals into unity; and these are three: first, as the basis for the other attributes, the fact that pyramids are solids; second, that they have flat bases bounded by straight lines; and third, that they have triangular sides meeting in a point. A fourth step is required to bind these three common attributes into the unity pyramid, and a fifth to infer the purpose in the form.

First step, leading to the generalization of the attribute solid.

1. Observing the manifold variety of individuals before the pupil, and those imagined by him.
2. Abstracting the attention from many other attributes and fixing it on the attribute, three dimensions — solidity.
3. Comparing and contrasting, finding all the differences consistent with the likenesses.
4. Generalizing the attribute of solidity, — "These objects are solids."

Second step, leading to the generalization of the attribute, having a flat base bounded by straight lines.

1. Observing again the diversity of individuals.
2. Abstracting the attention from all the other attributes and parts, and fixing it on the base.
3. Comparing and contrasting bases, finding all the likenesses and the differences consistent with them.
4. Generalizing the attribute under consideration, — "These solids have flat bases bounded by straight lines."

Third step, leading to the generalization of the attribute, bounded by triangles meeting in a point.

1. Once more, observing the individual pyramids.
2. Abstracting the attention from all other attributes and parts and fixing it on the sides.

3. Comparing and contrasting to find likenesses, and all the differences consistent with them.

4. Generalizing the common elements in the sides, — "These sides are triangles meeting in a point."

Fourth step, resulting in a synthesis of the three foregoing elements into the unity pyramid, and the formation of the definition.

1. Observing individuals as a whole, the attention not directed to any one element.
2. Comparing and contrasting pyramids
    a. With other known mathematical forms; as a cone, a cube, etc., comparing in the three points generalized.
    b. With each other, finding as many differences as possible so that essentials only remain.
    c. With forms of nature in which the essential elements of the mathematical pyramid are greatly obscured, noting the essential and the non-essential attributes; as, in a pile of oranges, a hill, a church spire, a paper weight, a tent, a tree, etc.
3. Generalizing all points of likeness, — "These objects are solids, having flat bases bounded by straight lines, and triangular sides meeting at a point." Then, the name pyramid having been given, "A pyramid is a solid," etc.

Fifth step, inferring the unity of all the attributes to mean the one attribute of stability; the purpose of the form. This attribute should be applied to historical pyramids, and to pyramidal objects. With this attribute in mind, the pyramid should be transformed by the poetic imagination into a spiritual type of a will holding firm against the opposing forces of life. Tennyson says of the Duke of Wellington: "He stood four-square to all the winds that blew," *i.e.*, withstood all the evil influences incident to his exalted position. The pupil will easily, with proper suggestions, transform himself into a pyramid, and state instances of how he could withstand this, that, and the other force directed against his character; just as the pyramid could withstand the forces striving to overturn it. This should be pushed out into the details of the pupil's experience until he feels broadly grounded, like the pyramid, against whatever would overthrow him; thus making the pyramid not merely an intellectual concept but a positive force in his ethical life. The best moral instruction is not that given by special lessons, but that which organizes into the movement of thought in every lesson.

Means in the Movement — *As a whole.* — Since the movement as a whole is that of thinking the diversity of individual pyramids into the unity of the idea pyramid, and since this movement is based on the observation of individuals, a striking diversity of individuals must be provided for the lesson, — pyramids of all sorts of material, forms, sizes, and colors; also forms supplied by the imagination. If the forms supplied were all of one material, form, size, and color, the pupil's generalization would bring into unity attributes foreign to the idea pyramid;

as, wood, slim, ten inches high, and yellow. The individuals must have such differences that each will cancel a non-essential attribute in another. For instance, if it is not essential that the straight lines bounding the base should be equal, some of the pyramids must have bases with equal sides and some with unequal. The least number of individuals to be supplied will be determined by the number of non-essential attributes to be canceled. And this must be done not only that unity alone among pyramids may remain, but that this unity may be seen in all its richness of diversity. The pupil must search for the confusing and endless variety of differences consistent with the common attributes of the pyramid. The concept is a consciousness of differences in unity; without differences there is no concept; nothing but a mere abstract.

Suppose now the pupils to be standing around a table on which the pyramids are placed; then the conditions for effective observation are completed. While there is no option as to the mental act required, the devices may vary greatly. The pupils might have remained at their desks, and each have been supplied with a proportionate part of the pyramids. The position of the class which will, under the conditions, secure the most effective observation and comparison and contrast determines the teacher's choice. This illustrates how the rational use of devices rests on the consciousness of the mental experience desired.

Means to the steps in the movement. — To generalization of attribute, solid.

1. "Point to three dimensions in one of the objects before you." (This done repeatedly, including objects of the same form imagined in empty space.)
2. "Take two objects." "Show differences." "Show three dimensions in both." (This done repeatedly.)
3. "What differences are found?" "What likeness in all?" (Ch.) "Three dimensions; therefore, they are all solids."

Means, to generalization of attribute, flat base bounded by straight lines.

1. "Touch the base of a solid." (This done repeatedly to fix attention on the base.)
2. "Apply edge of ruler to the base." (Many times by each pupil with different solids.) "Pass hand over base." "Look along base." (Both repeatedly done.) "Apply bases of one to another." (Done often.) (Ch.) "The bases of these solids are flat." "Again, apply bases of one to another and state differences." (Ch.) "They differ in size and shape." "Kind of lines, straight or curved, bounding base." (Ch. after examining many solids report) "The lines bounding the base are straight lines." "Take one of the objects and measure each edge of the base." (Repeatedly done till inequality in length of sides is noted.) "Take two of the objects and tell likeness and difference in bases." (Repeatedly done.)

3. "What kind of bases have these objects?" (Ch.) "These objects have flat bases bounded by straight lines."

Means, causing the generalization concerning the sides.
1. "Point to all the sides of one of the solids; of another," etc.
2. "Point out differences between the sides of solids." "The likenesses." (These acts repeated frequently.)
3. "These solids have what kind of sides?"
4. "Take a solid." "Put finger on the point of one triangle; on point of another," etc. (Ch.) "The triangles meet in a point."
5. "Tell what you know about the sides of these solids." (Ch.) "The sides of these solids are triangles meeting in a point."

Means, causing the synthesis of the common attributes into the unity of the pyramid.
1. "Tell what is true of all the objects before you." (Ch.) "The objects are solids having flat bases with straight edges and triangular sides meeting in a point."
2. "These objects are called pyramids." (The word pronounced and spelled.) "What is a pyramid?" (Ch.) "A pyramid is a solid," etc.

These means have been stated fully enough and carried far enough to illustrate how devices conform to the mental movement to be produced. A mechanical teacher uses means without a consciousness of their relation to the activity to be stimulated; or, rather, the devices are not consciously determined by that activity. Skill in giving directions, asking questions, and supplying conditions depends directly on skill in discerning the phases of mental movement required in learning the object under consideration. The teacher who, in the act of teaching, feels in close touch with the pupil's experience in learning, will, quick and true as instinct, light upon the fit direction or proper turn of question. Therefore, the study of the art of questioning and using devices must be based in the mental processes of the pupil.

Educational Value of the Process. — The teaching of any lesson should produce an effect on each of the three powers of the mind — the intellect, the sensibility, and the will. It is a serious mistake to hold that the subject of instruction is chiefly intellectual, and that only now and then something arises to quicken the emotions and to prompt to resolution. The mind is a unit, and the entire soul must be addressed in every lesson. The proposition in geometry, as well as the poem, should delight the heart and prompt to new issues of life. The simple intellectual truth, that five and five are ten, is warm with emotion and charged with ethical force, when wielded by the efficient teacher.

In teaching the pyramid, the teacher must be conscious that he is stirring all the powers of the soul to the end of free and virtuous life. The steps as they were outlined suggested only intellectual activity; but these when properly stimulated, are interfused with the emotions of the learner, which gives to life new impulse and higher tendency. The plan of the lesson cannot exhibit the feelings and tendencies, as it does the intellectual movement; but their presence must be secured through the mental steps, and their value noted in stating the educative power of a lesson. In stating the value of the lesson on the pyramid, it is clear that it must be stated in terms of all the powers of the mind. The teacher who stimulates only cold thought by means of the pyramid — if such is possible — loses at least two-thirds of its value to the student.

1. First, what is the intellectual value of the exercise? As to *knowledge* the pupil gains the idea pyramid. But what does this mean? One answer might be, that he is expected to know that object; and that he may be asked about it sometime, perchance in the examination; but the true answer is, that this new idea is an organ of knowing to aid him in mastering the thought of both the physical and moral worlds. The physical world is a world of form, and he will, in thinking it, impose upon it his new type of form. He will see pyramids in myriads of objects, and thus facilitate knowing their forms. And too, it is a type in the moral world, as already pointed out.

As to *discipline*, accurate, thorough, and methodical observation is cultivated. This has its value in every phase of the pupil's intellectual life. He lives in a world of forms; and his mastery of them is conditioned on thorough and systematic observation. Correct habits of observation are essential to full intellectual life; and in teaching the pyramid, the teacher is to be conscious, by that means, of forming those habits which are to be constant and determining factors in all the pupil's intellectual activity.

But a still more fundamental structure of thought is secured through the requirement of thinking the great diversity of individual pyramids into the unity of a single idea, pyramid. This grasping of the little world of pyramids into unity is the same activity in kind, but of lower degree, which grasps the separate phenomena of the world into the unity of the universe; and this is the ultimate problem of the intellect. The intellectual movement in this lesson is a type of the fundamental movement in gaining any knowledge whatever; and the teacher who, in teaching this lesson, is not conscious of training the mind in this fundamental and universal form of activity has not risen to the educational point of view from which come guidance and inspiration.

2. While this lesson would generally be considered a purely intellectual activity, it should arouse a high state of *emotion*. This would be taken as a matter of course in a reading lesson; or, perhaps, in a history lesson. But every activity necessary to grasp an object is accompanied by its own inherent emotion — an intellectual delight arising from the activity itself. The moment the child begins to detect unity amidst the confusion of differences among the pyramids, a strong current of pleasure sets in. Bain calls it "the flash of agreement." The strength of emotion aroused is a fairly true index of the clearness,

distinctness, and firmness of the intellectual activity grasping the unity of the objects.

Now, this intellectual feeling awakened by means of this object may seem a small matter; but let it be remembered that every time an intellectual feeling is awakened the pupil becomes the more able to rise above the low level of sensuous and sensual pleasure into the purer realm of spiritual life; into the life of pure ideas. Certainly a large problem for the teacher is that of loosening the grasp of sensuous feeling, and thus giving freedom to the higher spiritual life; and a potent means to this end is the awakening of intellectual emotion by means of just such lessons as may be given on the pyramid. The teacher must so train the pupil that he will find his highest joy in the life of thought. To this end, every object must be so presented as to make him feel that joy. Is it too much to ask of the teacher that he be conscious, in a lesson like the foregoing, of the opportunity to substitute pure spiritual emotions for enslaving, sensuous feelings? How much it would add to the pleasure of teaching if the teacher were, in the act of teaching, conscious of realizing, to however small a degree, such a glorious and far-reaching result as above described!

But this object, as is the case, perhaps, in all others, has not had its full effect on the learner until it arouses his æsthetic emotion. This feeling is awakened when he finds himself reflected in the object; when he transforms it into a type of his own life. So straight, so true, so clean-cut, so upward-tending — the very embodiment of character and the aspiration of the soul. He delights in it because it mirrors to him his true, ideal self. So fine a sentiment is little demanded by this utilitarian age of education ; but the soul of the child is pleading for it, and has reasons deeper than the utilitarian knows of. I wish this were the place to insist more fully on the duty of the teacher to awaken æsthetic emotions by every object which the mind of the learner touches. The teacher should leave no object under consideration as a cold thing of mere thought relations ; but should cause the pupil to make it glow by the power of his imaginative sentiment. I challenge any one to present a higher, or even a more practical, educational effect than the habit and the power of transforming every object coming before the attention into something beautiful and divinely true. A revelation and an inspiration will come to the teacher who will strive earnestly to apply this suggestion to the daily lesson, however commonplace and matter-of-fact be the object considered.

3. But how does this lesson appeal to the *will?* Certainly not in a way to cause some definite resolution and action, as that proposed by an oration. But there is will in the form of life-tendency. The pupil has had an enjoyment of truth ; and to that extent, has become a truth lover, and, therefore, has a tendency to be a truth seeker Have we not the faith that every lesson changes in some way the current of life? Shall the teacher not hold himself responsible in every lesson, for strengthening the tendency to seek truth, beauty, and virtue ? In general and abstract talk we speak of the character-forming power

of education: but so few of us bring ourselves to the concrete faith in the act of teaching the lesson before us. We do not feel that character tendencies are forming under our touch. Here the teacher may reach the true inspiration point. Inspiration comes in the consciousness of realizing ideals. The true teacher has set up an ideal of character to be attained in the pupil by his teaching; and when he feels his ideal being realized in his teaching act he experiences that elation which always accompanies the realization of ideals. The teacher thus finds himself in his work, just as the pupil finds himself in the pyramid. He thus puts, not simply his time, but his life in his work; can live in it, and not simply by it.

For the sake of clearness and emphasis, before taking up the universal element, a more condensed illustration of the teaching process may be added.

Suppose that a first-reader class have learned the word *boy*, and are now to learn its plural, *boys*.

The Mental Process. — *The process as a whole.* — The nearest related knowledge being that of the spoken words *boy* and *boys*, and that of the printed word *boy*, the movement as a whole is from these ideas to the idea of the printed word *boys*.

Steps in the process: —
  1. Seeing the word;
  2. Imagining the meaning back of the form;
  3. Comparing image with that of the singular form;
  4. Comparing form with the singular form;

5. Inferring that the power of *s* makes the difference in the images.

Means in the process:—

1. Presenting word to the eye on chart or blackboard.
2. Tell the class the word pointed to is *boys*.

(Here the teacher utilizes their knowledge of the idea and the spoken word *boys*.)

A pupil is asked to show what the word means, and he brings two boys to the front. Another is asked to show the meaning, and he presents three or four boys. This continued until all the boys in the room are presented at once; and, by the same process, the class are pressed till they image back of the word all the boys in the town; in the county; in the state; in the United States; in the world. Thus they will be made to feel the wonderful compass of the word.

3. The class should now show alternately what the word *boy* and the word *boys* mean; and conclude with a statement of difference in meaning.
4. Ask pupils to point to the letters which are alike; to that which is different.
5. With the word *boys* before the class, require the pupils to form the image. Now erase the letter *s* and require the image. This repeated till pupils feel the power of the letter to cause the imagination to compass all boys. Now call for the change which the letter *s* makes in the word *boy*, and the conclusions sought will be reached.

Note that while the mental steps are fixed, the means used may vary. The means here given are only to suggest how they must conform to the mental process to be produced. Again, all skillful use of means is conditioned on a ready and accurate perception of the mind's movement in learning.

Educational Value of the Process.—*Intellectual.*—A *knowledge* of the power of the letter *s*. Not a knowledge of the form of the letter simply, although this would be secured, if not known before; but the effect of the letter on the word *boy*. At first this seems to be a small matter; but it is a new organ of knowledge to them. They will apply the idea of that power to all other plural forms. It is an entering idea into whatever feature of a word varies its meaning—into inflection in general.

As to *discipline*, accurate observation of words; and this extends to all objects. This may be the first time the pupils have looked a word squarely in the face. There is, also, the training to put the full and definitely bounded idea back of the word. Usually only vague and blurred images float before the mind; so that while the eye is trained to see the word definitely, the imagination is exercised on the definite image which the word symbolizes. The pupil is thus trained to look through forms to meaning; through the clothes to the man; below appearances to realities. The most fundamental and pervasive form of mental life is that of reading behind phenomena the spiritualities on which they rest; of looking through the physical heavens to the glory of God which they declare. The teacher is not fully prepared to teach this lesson until his own mind has been transformed by some such process as that required in reading Carlyle's "Sartor Resartus," in which Carlyle, by successive removals of the outer husk and show of things, discloses the soul beneath,—until, "In a word, he has looked fixedly on Existence, till, one after the other, its earthly hulls and garnitures have all melted away; and now, to his rapt vision, the interior celestial Holy of Holies lies disclosed." In teaching the word *boys* the teacher is stimulating in the pupil the same fundamental form of thought, in an elementary way, as that required by the highest reach of philosophic mind. Would it not be the inspiration of a teacher to conduct the little process from this universal eminence? And has the teacher any professional right to teach this lesson without being conscious of, at least, some of the sky that bends over it? Further, the learning of this word affords a good exercise in complex comparison and contrast. The pupil must hold two images and two forms, while noting likenesses and differences in each. This form of activity constantly recurs in all thinking, and discipline in it must be an object of constant endeavor on the part of the teacher. The training to make definite the relation of cause and effect is clearly secured in this exercise.

Emotional. — The emotion cultivated is an intellectual one: that arising from the free exercise of the imagination, and the delight on discerning the power of the letter. While the steps enumerated are intellectual ones, emotion necessarily accompanies them. Not one of the steps can be taken without yielding a corresponding delight to the faculties. The emotion reaches its climax on discerning the great power of the letter *s*, the cause and effect relation. This is accompanied by pleasure which the free activity of the imagination brings in figuring the compass of the idea. Every lesson carries with it its own inherent source of pleasure. This lesson would be poorly taught if the pupil did not glow with feeling through the process; and the degree in the warmth of feeling would fairly well indicate the teacher's skill; that is, if the pleasure arises from the full and free activity in thinking the word, and not from some extraneous and illegitimate source. It cannot be too often nor too strongly insisted upon that the teacher must ever rely on the full, natural, and helpful activity of the pupil on the object under discussion for the pupil's deepest interest and highest reward; and not on the intrusion of some novel and exciting affair which lies outside of the legitimate line of thought.

Volitional. — This lesson does not necessarily prompt to any definite resolution, but it should confer life tendency. The pleasure which arises from the experience of truth, from the life of thought, will incline the student to truth seeking. If the life tendency is the same after the lesson as before, the question would arise, Why teach the lesson? The lesson warms to the glow of feeling which is finally to be kindled into a flame of passion for truth. The teacher is not prepared to teach this lesson until he sees clearly and feels fully the universal meaning in the direction of truth and virtue. The lesson is fraught with power for good, if the pupil's mind is naturally and fully exercised upon the object under consideration; if the whole soul — intellect, sensibility, and will — enters into the exercise. To substitute intellectual life for sensuous life is a great educational problem, and it is quite obvious that this lesson may be made a strong force in that direction.

Gain in Lesson Planning.

In conclusion, it may be insisted on that, so far as possible, all lessons should be prepared as in the foregoing. The reader will at once recoil at the thought of the immense labor thus imposed. If a teacher has twenty lessons per day and two hours must be spent on sketching each lesson, there will be but little time left for social duties and general reading. But this is no argument against the idea of thus preparing the lesson; for ideals must not be put aside because they cannot be realized. If so, what then would become of ideals of character? But it can be easily shown that such preparation is the only economical use of time; and that the reward is commensurate with the labor.

Such preparation inspires the teacher with the lesson; and he approaches the class with delightful anticipations of realizing an ideal which strives within him as a result of his carefully planned work. He has idealized the pupils' experience in gaining the point to be presented; represented to himself how the pupils would think and feel in their movement in grasping the thought; how this and that device would affect their activity; and thus an eagerness arises to see in the real process what has been brooded over in idea. Such a teacher approaches the recitation flushed with interest; and, by the law of sympathy, the pupils catch the spirit, and teacher and pupils fuse together in a glow of interest; and this insures that undivided attention and full activity which marks the highest degree of skill in teaching. This alone would reward the teacher's effort. It is worth all the commonplace rules on securing attention and interest. The teacher who makes no such study must continue to be the drudge instead of becoming the inspired artist.

Such a preparation of the individual lesson is the only sure means of growth in professional knowledge and skill. It is easy and customary to read books of pedagogy to no avail; the thought presented is held off at arm's length; it does not become a part of the concrete teaching life. As much as we boast of our study of psychology, it has helped the teacher but little. It is read, and then placed upon the shelf as if it had nothing to do with the real business in hand. Now, such a preparation as here insisted on would force the teacher to feel that psychology is the very breath of life in every teaching act. In the preparation of every lesson, the psychology must be kept at the right hand. The mental processes constituting the particular lesson to be given must be traced out, classified, and organized. The psychology of each lesson must be brought into consciousness. This solves the problem of interesting the teacher in psychology.

That this is the only sure approach to real, substantial pedagogy appears in this way : Suppose that a teacher should make out the mental process of learning, say, the noun ; and then another of the adjective, and so on through the subject, marking educational values in all cases. At this point, let the teacher reflect on all that has been done, and generalize all the processes and values into the pedagogy of grammar. Would not this method put to shame our ordinary talk about methods in teaching grammar ? Let this work be carried through all the subjects ; and then the teacher is prepared to construct a real science of education out of concrete experience. There is no other way in which this can be done. The notorious contradiction between fine talk on education and cheap practice would be canceled. The science of education would then have a real concrete meaning ; while the art would be stimulated and guided by a consciousness of universal law. Let the teacher, therefore, who is ambitious to grow in pedagogical theory and art begin with the analysis of the individual lesson before him ; and, by a long series of careful observations and generalizations, establish higher and still higher laws till a highly organized science has been reached. Is not this the scientific method, and therefore correct ? This would convert the ordinary labor of the school-room into a systematic study of pedagogy; whereas we usually teach school all day and then at spare hours study, as a distinct matter, some book on teaching. Work thus done is good ; but how much would it be reinforced if each lesson pressed the teacher out into such work from the necessity of penetrating the lesson itself?

If the foregoing reasons do not justify the great labor of lesson planning, it is useless to add others which might be given. Before closing, however, it ought to be noted that the labor is not so great by far as at first appears. Twenty lessons of two hours each requires forty hours' work per day. Such is the economy of time in lesson planning that a teacher can do the forty hours' work in a day, allowing eight hours for sleep. Suppose the lesson on the word *boys* has been prepared as above, and to-morrow the word *girls* occurs, and the next day *birds*, and then follow, as will, many plurals in *s*. The preparation on the first word takes care of all such that follow. And not only of words forming their plurals by adding *s*, but of all plural forms. When the words *boxes, oxen, men, mice*, etc., occur, their treatment is the same. Thus the two hours' work takes care of the forty. The one preparation includes that for all plural forms, with the exception of one step, which may here be noted. After the pupil has met with a few plurals ending in *s* he will begin to understand that words are made to mean more than one by the addition of *s*. Whether or not the teacher direct this generalization, the pupils will be forced to it by the repetition of examples. But when a plural in *es* is met with, after taking the steps as noted in the word *boys*, the pupils will instantly feel a check to their hasty generalization. And so with each new plural ending, thus forming a tendency to caution in generalizing. When the pupils have had a wide experience with plural forms, say for two or three years, they should, on the ground of their experience, and not from book testimony, gather into a system the laws for forming plurals. Therefore, with the added step of comparison and contrast, and generalization, the lesson prepared on the word *boys* is the preparation for the many lessons to follow, extending at intervals through four or five years in the school course. And not only the lessons on plural forms; but on all inflected forms. The mental process to be stimulated in teaching the meaning of *ie* in the word *birdie* is the same as that required to learn plural forms. The preparation for teaching prefixes and suffixes is therefore the same as that for teaching the word *boys*. And further, as might easily be shown, the same mental movement runs through all work in grammar. Of course we should expect the fundamental preparation of any lesson to reach in some way every other lesson. The teacher who shuns such preparation will, in the haphazard way, use vastly more time in the same course of work. The only economical use of time is to do a thing fundamentally right.

But it is not gain to the teacher but to the pupil that concerns us. Unless the process described economizes his time and fosters his growth, no claim can be made for it. That it does both for him is obvious on a moment's reflection. Suppose, using again the lesson on plural forms, that the pupil begins this work of close observation, comparison and contrast, and generalization with plural forms as they occur in his first reader, and continues this through the third reader. At that time he will have completed what is usually just begun at that point. And note the difference in condition of mind between him and the one who is put through the elementary grammar on the same subject after the orthodox fashion — a week or two of formal drill on definitions and examples as given in the book. If two classes thus differently drilled should be asked how words are made to mean more than one, what would be the difference in the mental processes of giving the answer? A pupil in one class will hold his breath and with a dead tug of memory reproduce something given him; while the other will enter into his experience of the past four or five years, and by an original construction can write out in notebook all the forms that have come within his experience. This is original work; while the other accepts on faith what some one has given him, and answers by a process of mechanical memory and not out of the fullness of his own life. Again, if it be asked, Which form is most generally used? which next? etc., the boy of healthy mind will again enter into his past years of experience and can write an original statement of "rules and exceptions," while the other passively copies what he has been taught. The one appeals to the language itself, the only authority, and holds himself responsible through his own mental processes for reaching the truth; while the other appeals to authority and shuns all activity and responsibility. It has been said that the former process lessens the pupil's respect for authority; while the latter will cultivate that virtue. But the pupil cannot respect authority till he becomes authority himself. Suppose that the pupil who has had four years of intimate experience with language should, in his fifth year, while writing up the conclusions of his own prolonged investigation, be directed to consult Harvey or Swinton on the same subject. What would be his delight in finding that they had reached the same conclusions as himself; had pushed the matter a little further perhaps, but then they had been at it longer. He would at once appreciate from his own experience that those men had been patient and careful seekers after truth; and could readily appreciate them as authority, knowing what authority means. He would congratulate them on their eminent success as investigators in his own line and would take them unreservedly into his fellowship, and respect them as he does himself. Without self-respect in the search of truth there can be no respect for the authority of others.

If the nature of the teaching act is now clear, we are prepared to consider the universal laws which control that act. Since Means in teaching is grounded in and through the Experience of the pupil in realizing the Purpose, the philosophy of Means is necessarily involved in that of the two other elements of the teaching act, and needs, so far as the process of teaching is concerned, no further separate treatment.

AIM IN TEACHING.

DIVERSITY OF AIMS.

The end to be realized is the moving force in every process; hence aim in teaching is logically first to be considered. The end as idea in the mind of the teacher moves to its realization by means of the process of teaching. It is both first and last — first as idea and last as objective reality. "The first shall be last and the last shall be first." There can be no teaching without an aim; no good teaching without a definite, inspiring, and worthy aim.

It means much to say that the teacher must have a definite aim in each recitation; but I wish to insist that the conscious aim in each recitation should be a universal one. This is the only aim that has in it real potency. To have any definite aim, as merely to give the knowledge of the height of a mountain range, gives definite and organic movement to that particular recitation; but each lesson must be seen as coördinate with every other — must be seen in the light of the whole round of the pupil's life. Each wave of influence set up in the pupil's life circles out to the other shore; and the teacher must look far out in life would he note the true meaning, the full opportunity, and fearful responsibility of every teaching act. The teacher must know that each lesson has not only its limited and specific object in knowledge and discipline, but that the real object is life itself. In planning a lesson, the teacher must state that a given point of knowledge is to be taught and that certain mental faculties are to be called forth; but unless he has traced out the ultimate bearing of such knowledge and such activities he has no reason for giving the knowledge or stimulating the activities.

This brings us to that most vital question in education — the true, or universal, aim in teaching. Not true simply as set over against false, but true in the sense of highest and most comprehensive; that aim which, in its realization, carries with it all lower aims. Many and diverse are the worthy results which education secures; but there is one end which brings into unity and harmony all the others. To seek directly the diversity of lower ends dissipates energy and defeats effort. Lower ends are most effectively secured by seeking the one true and essential end. What then, is this highest good of education?

Putting aside the false aims of vanity, such as polish for the social circle, preparation to hold positions of honor and notoriety, and the celebrity which comes from the mere display of learning and research, educational effort moves in two main and worthy channels: the one toward man's physical, the other toward his spiritual, good. Man seeks two ends in life: animal happiness and spiritual worthiness. Accordingly, education must serve in these two directions. It is the practical added to the culture aim; physical freedom *versus* spiritual freedom.

Of these two purposes in teaching, only an insignificant minority award the higher place to spiritual growth, the vast majority holding that education is a means to a livelihood, either in the business or in the professional world. While our philosophy of life regards thrift as the greatest blessing, our fundamental assumption in education must be that it should seek an external good rather than an internal condition of soul. Whatever culture is conferred through knowledge and discipline is for the sake of the industries and professions, and not for the good of the soul thus cultured. When the young man contemplates leaving home to seek higher education, the current question is, "What are you going to make of yourself?" thinking that but one kind of answer is possible, and that in terms of a vocation. By the vast majority, education is assumed, without question, to be instrumental to "getting on in the world," and nothing more. So ingrained is this into our habit of thought that intelligent people generally show surprise when any other view of the case is suggested. Everywhere in conversation, on the street, in the car, in the social circle, in associations of teachers, and even among scientists, whose professed aim is truth for truth's sake, there is implied the utilitarian end as the ground of education. Ruskin complains of the same thing in

England. He says in the many letters he receives from parents asking advice concerning the education of their sons and daughters he uniformly finds the thought of advancement in life; of something that will put a better coat on the boy's back; that will enable him to ring with confidence the bell at the double-belled doors, and after awhile to have a double-belled door of his own.

Now, all this is easily accounted for. Each nation puts into its educational thought what is uppermost in its life. Instance China, Athens, Rome. The western world is in stern conflict with its physical environment. Hence educational forces are enlisted in the accumulat on of material power; in securing the physical freedom of man.

It certainly ought not to be urged that physical freedom is an unworthy aim in education; for man's spiritual freedom is largely conditioned on his physical freedom. But that physical comfort and happiness constitute the sole aim, or the highest one, needs to be seriously questioned. Rousseau thus emphasizes the other side: "In the natural order of things, all men being equal, the common vocation to all is the state of manhood; and whoever is well trained for that, cannot fulfill badly any vocation which depends upon it. Whether my pupil be destined for the army, the church, or the bar, matters little to me. Before he can think of adopting the vocation of his parents, nature calls upon him to be a man. How to live is the business I wish to teach him. On leaving my hands he will not, I admit, be a magistrate, a soldier, or a priest; first of all he will be a man."

Since education is both a physical and a spiritual good, there are two ends to be reached by the same process. This cannot be done if the ends are antagonistic; but may be done if one is higher and the other lower, — if one is more fundamental, so that, when it is secured, the other will be realized in the process. The warfare between industrial and cultural education recognizes opposition between the ends sought. But there is no such opposition; instead, there is essential harmony. By focussing the effort on the fundamental end, the other will be effectively secured; and much more effectively than if the lower end be directly sought. If the needs of the soul be administered unto, the utilitarian ends of life will be much more surely and truly realized than if the latter end be sought directly. If, in the act of teaching, the teacher holds firmly in consciousness, and is guided by, the spiritual growth of the child, the best possible thing will be done for a successful career in life.

We must keep in mind that what is popularly known as practical education is the most impracticable. Power to think, to adjust the mind to the realities in the world, to reach true conclusions from carefully discriminated data; strongly developed and refined sensibilities; and an ethical nature fully aroused — these are in the line of a truly practical education. Book-keeping is not the immediate nor the fundamental qualification of a clerk; nor skill in measuring corn-bins and in computing interest the first necessity of a good farmer. In the eternal fitness of things, that which makes a man a man supplies the fundamental necessity for vocations. A clerking man or a farming man is not so serviceable as a man clerking or a man farming. We rely too much on the immediate outfit, and not enough on those powers of mind and heart which make the man adequate to varying conditions and unexpected situations as they arise. This is the great weakness in the present system of preparing for the profession of teaching. Effective service can come only from a full-orbed manhood or womanhood enlisted in the service — men and women, who, from their enlarged powers of mind and heart, can not only contrive the means to meet the immediate necessity of instruction, but, from the larger range of spiritual life, feel the real needs of the life they seek to unfold.

Whatever the diversity of views as to the purpose of teaching, it arises from the diversity of views as to the nature and purpose of life. If all had the same views of life, there would be unity of aim in teaching. All agree that education is to aid in living — to further life's interest; that whatever subject and method of instruction aids most in life should be selected. But when asked, What is living? What is life? the apparent simplicity of the problem vanishes. The true and comprehensive aim in teaching is found in the nature and purpose of life.

AIM FOUND IN NATURE OF LIFE.

Whether physical or spiritual, life is change. There may be change without life, but there is no life without change. The change is a definite course from an idea to its realization, analogous to the mechanical changes in the world of man's creation. Everything made by man exists first in idea, then in objective reality. The Brooklyn Bridge was first an idea, and then followed a series of changes which brought the idea into the external world of reality. Whatever man has brought to pass has moved from a subjective idea to an objective one — from the ideal to the real.

There is a similar change in the plant world. The idea, or potential oak, is in the acorn. Life in the oak consists of a series of changes by which the potential oak becomes the actual oak. But the analogy to the mechanical world holds no further. The changes from the idea to the objective reality in the mechanical world are produced by a force external to the changing object. External forces and appliances brought into objective reality the idea Brooklyn Bridge. But the force which urges to the realization of the oak is in the germ itself. External conditions must favor, yet the oak takes an active part in its own realization. The vital force bursts the acorn, pushes downward and upward, grappling with the earth beneath, and stemming the storm above, until it becomes the strength and majesty which were only potential at the outset. The grain of corn, pressed by crust and clod, pushes and twists and turns, until it finally wedges through to air and sunlight. After a day of seeming dalliance with the summer wind, it bends under the wealth of fruit which it was destined to produce. The poet thinks that —

> "Every clod feels a stir of might,
>   An instinct within it that reaches and towers,
> And groping blindly above it for light,
>   Climbs to a soul in grass and flowers."

This self-urgency in the plant is unknown in the mechanical world. While in both there is change from the idea to its realization, yet the force in a mechanical change is external to that which changes; while in a vital change the force is in the changing object — a blind self-struggle for the realization of its innermost nature and true being. The same is true of animal life. While to mere vital force instinct is added in the animal, for the purpose of the illustration, we need note only that the urgency which brings about the changes called life is within the changing object: —

> "To-day I saw the dragon-fly
> Come from the wells where he did lie.
> An *inner impulse* rent the veil
> Of his old husk: from head to tail
> Came out clear plates of sapphire mail."

The little bird with tired wing lines her nest, and with patient purpose sits on her eggs, while the "heart in her dumb breast flutters and sings" in the blind faith of accomplishing that whereunto she was sent. Ever there is something that urges. The eagle knows not why, but he laboriously mounts upward, and frets if chained to the low earth to feed on unworthy prey. The wounded eaglet —

> "Rests, deep-sorrowing,
> On the low rock beside the stream.
> Up to the oak he looks,
> Looks up to heaven.
> While in his noble eye there gleams a tear."

Wherever there is plant or animal life there is a force that pushes outward and upward, contending with whatever stands between the living object and the realization of its true nature. At any given moment a living thing has that nature within it which will destroy the present state of the object. The object is at war with itself. Its present real self is a bondage to its future ideal self. Yet the ideal could not rise except upon the ground of the real.

So far as it goes, physical life is a fit type of spiritual life; foreshadows it; is the prophecy of the higher life. Spiritual growth, too, is a series of changes from the ideal to its realization; and, too, the soul has within itself its own urgency to self-realization. Spiritual growth is a process of development under the innate force of the soul itself. As in the physical world, the possible crowds upon the real and displaces it with a higher phase of being. Spiritual life is a striving, an urgency, to self-realization. There is no soul but what is moved by the instinct of its destiny; it is its own prophecy and its own fulfillment.

Notwithstanding this fundamental likeness between physical and spiritual growth, there is an essential difference. The plant and the animal move to their realization without plan or purpose of their own. They do not foresee what they are to become; they cannot distinguish between the ideal and the real, by which they are what they are. But the soul in the process of growth is conscious of the distinction between the realized and the unrealized self. Man can project his possible self in idea; can think of himself as other than he is, which the highest forms of animal life give no signs of doing. This makes man a self — a person. What a man is to be is an object of interest to himself, prompting him to conscious effort to reach his highest good. This, and not the fact that he binds thoughts together in logical sequence, makes man a rational being; for animals show remarkable skill in logical connection. The parrot, in throwing aside a light nut, must do so in obedience to a logical syllogism: "Nuts that are light are not good for Polly; this nut is light; therefore, not good for Polly." But we have not the slightest evidence that Polly ever sets before herself an ideal parrot-hood to be the goal of her endeavor. If so, we should have schools for parrots; for schools are to help beings consciously realize some unrealized condition set up as an end. Education is conditioned on the fact of self-consciousness. If a man could not see himself as other than he is — see himself as he ought to be in contrast with his present condition — he could not be taught. Through self-consciousness man can determine himself; he is something more than a fated fact among the blind forces of nature; he is free to form his own life, and is to be held responsible therefore. Thus it is —

> "That men may rise on stepping-stones
> Of their dead selves to higher things."

In thus objectifying the soul to itself, the intellect, the objectifying power of the mind, renders its fundamental service in spiritual growth.

Consciousness of an unrealized self as in contrast with a present self is the fundamental and universal fact of human life. This consciousness has all shades of explicitness; but wherever there is a human soul, there is either dimly felt or distinctly grasped some spiritual good yet unattained. The dim life of the child is vaguely grasping at what it would become; it may be no more than wishing to be big like papa or mamma; yet it grasps at a future good, which is a prophecy of better things. Longfellow says : —

> "That even in savage bosoms
> There are longings, yearnings, strivings
> For the good they comprehend not;
> That the feeble hands and helpless,
> Groping blindly in the darkness,
> Touch God's right hand in that darkness
> And are lifted up and strengthened."

With advancing culture life becomes a definite object to the self; character is definitely and clearly seized; and all effort may be brought to bear on what the soul instinctively feels to be its highest good.

While the vision of a noble character floating before the mind is essential to spiritual growth, of itself it will not insure that growth. Man must be susceptible to the influence of that ideal; must be drawn irresistibly unto it. The emotional nature responds to the ideal which the reason sets up. We call it the feeling of worth; pride of character. Contemplating the ideal of life gives rise to a feeling of dissatisfaction with the present self — a feeling of unworthiness in presence of ideal worthiness. Other things equal, the greater the tension felt between the real and the ideal, the higher the character. Self-satisfaction is the evil of the age. There is little hope for him who is contented with his present attainment. A noble-minded, high-spirited youth is intoxicated with an ideal; and can find no peace till he is in direct pursuit of the highest good. Elated he continually commands himself, —

"Build thee more stately mansions, O my soul,
 As the swift seasons roll!
 Leave thy low vaulted past!
 Let each new temple, nobler than the last,
 Shut thee from heaven with a dome more vast,
 Till thou at length art free,
 Leaving thine outgrown shell by life's unresting sea!"

Man may have clearly before him a noble ideal and may be keenly alive to its influence, and yet not mount joyously to the stars. He is painfully conscious of a dead weight, which he must strive with might and main to overcome ; —

> "He knows a baseness in his blood,
> At such strange war with something good
> He cannot do the thing he would."

This requires the vigorous action of the third power of the soul, the will. Unless the strong arm of resolution reach forth and hold the ideal against every counter interest of life, the intellect will have created the ideal in vain, and the feeling of worth will be dissipated in air. The organic function of the three powers of the soul in the life process has now appeared. The intellect objectifies the self to the self — creates the character yet to be formed and opposes it to the present self; the emotions respond with a feeling of interest in the ideal set up — a feeling of unity between the present and the ideal self; while the will actively lays hold on the ideal and brings the present self into unity with the ideal set up. The last activity — the effort to hold to the true worth of the soul against the forces which strive to drag life downward — is the activity uppermost in consciousness, and makes life what we immediately feel it to be, a conscious striving to realize some unattained good.

Life is simple; it is choosing the ideal worth of the soul against every other interest that may clamor for recognition. The choice is to be made between two things only: the present, real self, and the future, ideal self; and in obedience to the doctrine that, "He that findeth his life shall lose it." This contains the whole law. The real and true life of the soul can be found only by losing the realized self, which always forms a bondage to the ideal to be obtained. Every choice in life is between these two selves; and one must necessarily be sacrificed to the other. The law of self-sacrifice means only that the lower self must be sacrificed to the higher. The true self is never to be sacrificed.

It thus appears that the law of life is internally given, and not externally imposed. It is necessary, during a low phase of moral development, to announce laws as if they derived their validity from external force and authority. "Thou shalt not steal," was, to the children of Israel, direct and external authority from heaven; and the state imposes this law on its subjects; yet every one who has risen to self-consciousness is aware that the law issues from his own nature. When a man steals a horse, the loss of the horse to the owner is a minor matter; the serious thing is the loss of the man who steals the horse. It is easy to see how one can afford to lose a horse; but impossible to think that any one can afford to be the thief. The right of property is ground for the state to impose laws against dishonest practices; yet a little reflection will convince every one that the law has its ultimate sanction within the individual on whom the law is imposed. His own worthiness forbids in more thundering tones than were ever state laws proclaimed, "Thou shalt not kill," because in so doing thou murderest thine own soul. The citizen rises into civil freedom as he recognizes that public laws are subjectively sanctioned; and that in rendering them obedience he is only obeying himself. The righteous man is not fretted by external authority, but lives under a law self-imposed. He is more concerned about being just to every man than that every man shall be just to him. When the young man, warmed with wine, boasts that this is a free country, he means only that there are no external laws to prevent him doing as he pleases in this chosen line of revelry; but he thus shows himself to be the sorriest of slaves, being beastly unconscious of, or indifferent to, a law within, which imposes the death penalty for high crimes against himself. He does not perceive that freedom is voluntary force against restraint, rather than the absence of restraint; and that true life is this freedom.

The life conflict is within the soul itself, and not with the horned monster of fable. The love of money may occupy against the feeling of the soul's highest good. They struggle for possession. Being antagonistic, they cannot coexist. This is all: the soul in conflict with its own content. It sets itself over against itself, and contends with its lower interests for the survival of that which the divine light of reason shows to be in harmony with the true self. It is a silent but heroic conflict in the only kingdom where man has rule; a conflict self-imposed by a soul resolute to establish its highest claims against the appetites, desires, impulses, prejudices, and whatever in the lower world contends for sway in the realm of man's being. It is truly a struggle of the soul with itself for the survival of the best within it. Whatever may be said of natural law in the spiritual world, here is a spiritual law which has no parallel in the natural world. In the natural world, objects struggle with external things only to survive; the fittest do; and these may be the best. But the animal does not struggle to survive because it is fittest or best; while the soul struggles with itself and for the survival of the best. When man loses his impulse to such a struggle, he crosses the line and becomes an animal; he is spiritually dead. So long as he strives, he is not lost; heaven will at last come to the rescue of his better nature.

Man struggles with external objects — with nature for mastery over its forces; with his fellow-man in the final arbitrament of the sword; but his real, sublime, heroic, life-and-death struggle is in his own subjective kingdom. Here is the world's real battle-ground. Here are fought the decisive battles — the Gettysburgs and Waterloos. Without noise and spectacle, yet here are the deeds of heroic valor and of noble self-sacrifice. During the conquest of Mexico, while the vast armies were set in battle, two men on the flat top of a high temple were planted in mortal combat. At the sublime moment when each was trying to dislodge the other from the dizzy height, the armies below caught the spectacle, forgot their warfare, and watched the issue. In the temple of man's heart is such a contest, and, could we behold it, we too would cease our warfare of daily duties and business life to watch the issue, — whether the soul, stimulated by its own sense of worth, will hold against some enemy planted to dislodge it from the temple of communion with its Maker.

Life's ideal heroic struggle is exhibited in its most perfect form in literature. In fact, all literature portrays the soul rising from death unto life — from its "dead self to higher things." Bryant's "Water-fowl" exhibits the soul rising above the disappointments and perplexities of life to the serenity of faith in a guiding Providence. The soul is dejected, and this means death. It must rally to new life; and this it does through faith in a guiding Providence, as revealed in the "Water-fowl." The hero, Donald Grant, in George McDonald's novel, finds his life threatened from disappointment in love. He entertains successfully the "irrepressible conflict," furnishing a true type of the life struggle. Not a struggle with some positive form of sin — a disappointment in love, a hard hit stunning his spiritual being — but requiring the same appeal to his sense of manhood in order to gain victory over the tribulations of life. Instead of death there was more life and a heavenly birth, such as comes to every man who stimulates his pride of worth and overcomes in the hour of trial. "The cure o' a' ill's nather mair nor less nor mair life," and Donald Grant thronged his life pulse with all the noble thoughts and sentiments of his past life, and prophecies of the future, — all that he had been, all that he hoped to be, — as every youth must do who triumphs over the sins and ills of life; and happy will be that youth whose richness and fullness of spiritual life will tide him over the shallows and breakers of his out-going voyage.

It was by such means that Ralph, in the "Hoosier School-master," fought so well. He had a struggle alone and in the dark, — not a hand-to-hand contest with a robber, — our struggles seldom are, — not a struggle in the dark with a hair-breadth escape through a trap-door such as makes the hair bristle, but a real, terrible struggle in the dark, whether he should follow the dictates of love or live to a higher life. In the wakeful, tedious hours of night, he stirs every noble sentiment of the heart to come to his rescue, — he thinks of his mother's words, the old Bible stories, his youthful aspirations after nobility of spirit, the solemn resolutions to be true to his better self, the vision of the supreme value of a true character, "the memory of a travel-worn Galilean peasant, hungry, sleepy, weary, tempted, tried like other men, but having a strange divine victory by which everything evil was vanquished at his coming." All the angels of memory came flocking back to the rescue, and victory crowned the struggle ; and not only victory, "but what is better, strength." It was a real, awful struggle in the dark for the survival of the best. It was the spirit contending with the flesh ; the battle that every well endowed person must fight, and the victory that every soul must win — the victory of the soul over the tribulations of life.

This again is the typical battle of life ; the soul striving under the stimulus of its inherent worth, reinforced by the thronging in of every noble thought and sentiment that ever thrilled the mind and heart.

It must not be supposed that man is always wrestling with a strangling serpent of sin. He may be free from the ordinary forms of passion and appetite ; the evil temptations may have no power over him ; yet effort is required to rise to the fullest stature of man. He must still strive to become more·than he is. The youth has not simply to decide to withstand that which attacks him, but must energize himself to meet the highest claims life has upon him. Life is not merely the absence of wrong doing; it is noble effort. We are not to think that man should be never wrong; but that he should be ever nobly right. But in whatever form the striving appears, its nature is the same; it is produced by the aspiration of the soul to attain to its divinely appointed end, and is carried to a successful issue by ever consciously stimulating it by a deeper sense of personal worth and reinforcing it by a fuller sweep of spiritual life.

So far, it appears that the true purpose of teaching is to make the youth keenly sensitive to the soul's worth and to inspire him with a longing for what is truest, best, and most beautiful in life; to make him fully conscious of the nature of the struggle which he feels disturbing him, and to prepare him for victory by nourishing a "youth sublime on the fairy tales of science and the long results of time"; by stirring the mind with large and generous thoughts, and the heart with noble, inspiring sentiments; by opening up to him all the great thoroughfares of human thought and making him responsive to the world's harmony; by all that gives tone, vigor, and power to life; by whatever makes the even current of life full and strong, that there may be an overpowering reinforcement to rally in the hour of attack, and angels of memory to strengthen and comfort under the cares and burdens of life.

But the true aim must yet be more fully exhibited by viewing —

Life as an External Process.

Life as an inner, conscious striving to realize possibilities is impossible without a correlative external process. The subjective process carries with it an objective process. Man cannot find his life within himself. This is found only in touching the thought and spirit of the world objective to the self. The individual must come in touch with the universal.

There is an inner vital process in the oak by which it realizes itself; but this inner process would not be possible were it not for the external process by which the tree comes in touch with and takes into itself the substance of which its life is built. The internal life processes of a bird are supported by answering external activities. Its walking, running, flying, searching for food, etc., administer unto the internal necessities. All internal vital processes are thus supported by activities adjusted to external ends. Thus physical life has an inner and an outer process organically related, each making possible the other.

The inner process becomes more complex and involved in passing upward into the higher forms of physical life; and the external process becomes correspondingly more complex and involved. The inner process of life in the oak is very simple when compared with that in the bird; and so likewise is the external process in the one simple when compared with that in the other. The oak is fixed to one place, and can appropriate only that which impinges on its surface. It passively waits on the circulation of air and moisture to bring it nutriment. But the bird actively puts under contribution a wide range of territory to sustain the necessities of its inner life. The widely extended and diversified activity in this case is proportioned to the more highly complicated internal activity. The ascending scale of physical life is determined by the ever widening circle of external activity. The lion can put under contribution a vast territory for his physical comfort and necessity, while the sponge is fixed to the area of its own body. This fact marks the grade of the lion's life over that of the sponge.

In the same way we note man's superiority as an animal. While primitive man was as restricted in physical freedom as the animal, through the progress of civilization he has put the entire globe under contribution for his individual comfort and happiness. The elements that once enslaved him, he now bids do his service. He can live in all parts of the world by modifying the heat of summer and the cold of winter, through the adjustment of clothing and shelter. He can "make Canada as warm as Calcutta." All parts of the world are compelled to feed and clothe him. The ocean, which for thousands of years imprisoned him, he now forces to be his liberator. He girts the continent with iron rails, and loosens the grasp of space and time. The lightning which threatens him, he tames and sends on trusty missions the world over. He bids the uttermost parts of the earth minister unto him, and it is done. When the animal or the savage desires some object of physical good, he must go and lay hold upon it; but civilized man, in physical ease and luxury by his fireside, commands the multiform blessings of earth, and the North and the South, the East and the West, and the lands beyond the sea, empty their comforts at his feet. Man's external physical life is infinitely more varied, complicated, and extended than is that of the lower animals. He has, beyond all comparison, the highest degree of physical freedom. By the aid of thought, he multiplies his natural physical power to overcome the pressure of his material environment and wrest it to his service. His locomotive power is increased twenty fold, and all fatigue removed. Through the invention and application of the manifold forms of the lever, the strength of arm by which he wrestles with the forces of nature has been surprisingly increased in power and variety of application. The voice is naturally limited to the range of a few paces; but by means of the telegraph and the telephone he speaks to the civilized globe. The microscope and the telescope come to the aid of limited vision, and bring to light the miracles of hidden worlds. The wonders wrought by labor saving machinery in securing man the prime requisites of life — food, clothing and shelter — need only be mentioned.

All this is civilization; by which is meant the degree of physical freedom man has attained through his arts, inventions, and industries.

Civilization is that form of life in which the activities of each man is strengthened by the combined activities of all. Thus is the miracle wrought. The race is a highly organized industrial unit. Each man lives by some specialized labor, and thus ministers to the wants of all; while he in turn is the recipient of every multiplied form of comfort arising from the diversified labor of others. The civilized world is a network of interdependencies. The shoemaker cannot fill an order without giving motion to the whole industrial world. Every line of industry must wait upon him to meet the necessities of his life which he himself cannot administer unto because of his own special occupation. The match factory, the iron mine, the stone quarry, the farm, the flouring mill, the saw mill, the store, the school, the state, the church, and so on without limit, are called into service because this man is a shoemaker: —

> "Ah! what a wondrous thing it is
> To note how many wheels of toil
> One thought, one word can set in motion!
> There's not a ship that sails the ocean,
> But every climate, every soil,
> Must bring its tribute, great or small,
> And help to build the wooden wall."

This triumph of physical freedom through arts and industries carries with it a great deal more than the physical freedom which belongs to the animal. Man's progress in physical freedom necessitates a substitution of intellectual life for physical life; for every step man takes in physical progress is taken through means devised by the intellect, — means requiring intensity of intellectual life by the impelling necessity of physical freedom, — that beautiful necessity which is a blessing in disguise, lifting man up against the dead weight of his life by forcing him to think, to feel, and to do. Our highly wrought civilization has come to be what it is under the highest spiritual tension of man, and has therefore wrought a higher result than was directly intended. Physical freedom is the conscious necessity which is the mother of invention; and this in turn gives increased power and freedom to thought. It requires a high degree of abstraction and generalization to adjust one's self to the complex relations of industrial life; and no better schooling can be given to the emotions and the will than that of being forced to harmonize one's self with the varied interests which coöperate for the good of the whole. In all of this there is manifested that divine economy which brings man to serve a higher end than the one immediately impressed on his attention. "All the world over, it is necessity that coerces us to the acquisition of the best things."

Unfortunately, however, physical freedom does not serve purely the interests of spiritual freedom. We have become manacled by that which serves to free us. Our time and energy, our spirit and buoyancy, are quite used up in the fever of what we call "getting on." To accumulate the means of life has become a pleasure, and the means an end; so much so that we cannot desist at the point of competency and turn our energies to a higher end — growth and culture of the soul. The means of life become the end of life; and our faith lays hold of nothing but meat and bread; rain, soil, and sunshine; trades and traffic; machinery, workshops, and industrial schools. We are on a dead strain to subjugate the powers of nature to purposes of individual comfort and happiness. The feverish energy to utilize the material forces about us prevents us from directing a portion of our time to purposes of spiritual life after providing physical sustenance. Civilization forestalls the ends of culture, and we will have to assert our own worth and dignity over that by which we live before we can mount into the upper air of light and liberty. While we boast of the nineteenth century as the triumph over material forces, we must not fail to see that this fact carries with it the other, namely, the spiritual absorption of the race in material interests. The fundamental assumption of American life is that the purpose of man is to subdue the physical earth. The infinite possibilities of the soul have no place in our plans. Most people act on the assumption that physical life is the only life, and animal happiness the true end of living. While this is not the avowed doctrine, it yet orders our conduct. To accumulate material resources and gain that power over the world which wealth confers is the end of all endeavor.

The assumption that the purpose of life is the attainment of physical freedom becomes necessarily the fundamental assumption as to the aim in education. It must serve the trades and industries; especially so in common-school education. Everywhere taxes are paid to this end. Education must be practical; a means to physical freedom, not to a condition of the soul. This is so obvious that surprise is awakened if any other end than the industrial one be suggested. But no matter as to the higher end now ; physical freedom is a worthy object of pursuit, and education a most potent means thereto. The relation of the common-school branches to it is quite obvious. It has been noted that man realizes his physical freedom through the form of industrial life — through the industrial unit called the civilized world. If all knowledge of arithmetic were at once taken away, the industrial unit is instantly broken. The shop and the bank must close ; the train must stop ; commercial intercourse becomes impossible ; and each man becomes instantly isolated, and, therefore, a savage, having to quit his vocation and supply every necessity directly by his own hand, receiving nothing from the combined effort of the world. If reading and writing were taken from us, the industrial network is broken and man again is out of touch with the race and must supply directly his every single necessity. No wonder we worship the three R's ! Among the educational changes proposed no one has ever been so bold as to think of striking out these subjects. Their value is felt to bear immediately and directly on the struggle for physical sustenance. The most illiterate appreciate their power unto physical freedom, if they do not always see their relation to righteousness. Of all subjects these are the most immediate to our every-day necessities ; and hence have the highest value placed upon them.

While not so obvious, the same result would follow if a knowledge of geography be removed. The earth is the physical basis of the industrial unit. Geography, simply as a knowledge of place, makes possible the world-combination. The earth, as a physical organism, bears a direct relation to the industrial organism. Geography, therefore, saves us from being savages, limited to the area which each could traverse on foot and to the use of that which each could supply with his own hand. Still less obvious is the relation of history to the physical struggle; and this accounts for its later appearance in the school course. And when it did appear its value was indirectly made out, thus: The study of history makes good citizens; good citizens regard the rights of property; my property is essential to my physical well being. Then the way was clear. For the same reason, physiology, too, appeared late. It came in on the score of health. A knowledge of hygienic laws saves from pain and the doctor's bill; and is not this physical freedom? Neither in this case nor in that of history was the life of the soul taken into account. Teachers still emphasize most the fact that history makes the orderly citizen, and that physiology is a matter of hygiene. When drawing is put into the school it is under the excuse of its being industrial. What it has to do with the growth of the soul does not occur to the tax-payer.

Thus the common-school branches are fundamental in the sense that without them our civilization would be impossible. They formulate and preserve the knowledge which conditions industrial life. Their bearing on our daily bread is felt to be immediate and direct; and their great value is unmistakably discerned. There is no other educational sentiment so deeply rooted, and no other so universally entertained. Physical comfort and happiness is the controlling aim in education; especially in the common-school phase of it. In the preceding pages it was urged that spiritual growth is the supreme object of school work. Yet none can deny that the school has a great work to do in preparing for the struggle of physical life. These two great and worthy aims are before us. How to reconcile and unify them is the next problem.

UNIFICATION OF AIMS.

The two great channels in which educational effort moves are the industrial and the cultural. Man is more conscious of the struggle to gain physical sustenance and power than of the struggle to realize ideals of character. Thus the industrial bearing of education is exalted above its spiritual power. The two kinds of education are set opposite as if to attain the one were to ignore the other. Common-school education is held to be merely instrumental, while the college confers liberal culture — liberal because freed from the industries and pursued for the good of the soul itself. Truth for truth's sake is the fundamental idea of the true university; while truth as a means of gaining a livelihood is the burden laid upon the public school.

No such distinction properly exists. There is one and the same supreme aim in both cases, the attainment of which carries with it every lower right aim; and the lower ends are most effectively secured by seeking the higher. While in the practical world of education there is great tension between these two ideals, in deepest truth there is nothing but organic harmony between them. Whatever is essential to spiritual growth prepares for industrial life and for securing physical freedom.

We have found a close analogy between physical and spiritual life. Physical life requires man to come into unity, by some external process, with the physical world about him; and the extent to which he can put under contribution that physical world for purposes of individual comfort and happiness marks the degree of physical freedom attained. This freedom is secured through the form of industrial life, by which the whole world is made into a complex unit of interdependencies. This unity is made possible by the knowledge formulated and preserved in the subjects of the school curriculum. Man's spiritual growth is conditioned on coming into unity with the thought and spirit of the world about him. His deeper, richer, fuller spiritual life depends on the enlargement of his spiritual horizon, by transmuting into the substance of his own thought the thought of the world into which he is born. This spiritual unity is analogous to the physical unity; and man is spiritually free to the extent to which he is one in thought, emotion, and purpose with the great thought in which he lives and moves and has his being. This unity, too, is made possible by pursuing the lines of study forming our school curriculum. There are not two classes of subjects — culture subjects and practical subjects. Whatever is requisite to participation in the physical life of the world is also requisite to spiritual participation.

But these ends are not coördinate and reversible. It is not a matter of indifference which is set up as the goal; for it will be found that spiritual requirements are supreme, and, when met, the lower physical good is secured in the process; and more effectively than by direct effort. This puts the common school and the university on the same plane. Both seek truth for truth's sake. Knowledge is its own end in one case as in the other. The common school is an institution of liberal culture; and the more thoroughly this end is secured the more substantial the equipment for the practical duties of life. If geography be so taught as to meet the spiritual necessity of the child, the best thing possible has been done in the interest of practical education. History best takes care of the practical question of citizenship by causing the pupil to feel the life of the past throbbing in his own; and this is just what the teacher brings to pass for the pupil's sustenance. Reading so taught as to awaken ideals in the pupil and to stimulate him to realize them is sure to answer best all the practical purposes of that subject. Whatever drill in arithmetic is best suited to give scope and power to the mathematical faculty, as culture itself demands, is exactly in the line of practical training. The truth thus vaguely stated must now be made to appear definitely through some detailed illustrations.

It has already been noted that the industrial unit, through which man achieves physical freedom, would be instantly destroyed were a knowledge of geography obliterated. The industrial world is a network of vital interdependencies encompassing the earth. A knowledge of the mathematical and physical earth is absolutely essential to the practical operation of the industrial organism. It has been noted also that man's spiritual growth is through unity with the thought and spirit of the world by which he is encompassed. Suppose a wall sky-high built up closely about the child's home, so that he cannot unite himself with what lies beyond, and the spiritual bondage will be tenfold more oppressive than his physical bondage resulting from ignorance of the world about him. What spiritual illumination, joy, and freedom, if the world could instantly burst on the thought of such a prisoner! — with the dizzy whirl of its immensity through space; with its vast forms of land and water, and the mighty forces that "heave the hill and break the shore, and evermore make and break and work their will"; with its hills, —

> "Rock-ribbed and ancient as the sun, the vales
> Stretching in pensive quietness between;
> The venerable woods — rivers that move
> In majesty, and the complaining brooks
> That make the meadows green; and poured round all,
> Old Ocean's gray and melancholy waste";

and everywhere the joy of murmuring life; and the teeming millions of men, "toiling, rejoicing, sorrowing," ever striving to ameliorate their present condition, sustained and animated by the inextinguishable hope of a better day. The world is a thought of God. It is not a dead mass of matter any more than the great organ of Westminster Abbey is the substance of wood and iron; but like the organ, a system of relations and forces — a stupendous organism — making melody to the ear trained to listen. In studying the earth, the student comes into unity with thought which lies beyond himself and is thus enlarged to the compass of that thought. The presence of the earth in consciousness is the enlargement and fulfillment of life to that extent. The pupil craves the living thought which is the earth, because this living thought is his other and true self. What would man sacrifice to see the earth in the fullness of its external features as they would be revealed to him, if by some means he could bring himself into every nook and corner of it! and how much more to know the secret laws of its organization, its final cause and method of operation! If, without any thought of its practical value, the teacher should cast about to find a subject to break the spiritual bondage of the child, geography would take its place as one of the fundamental branches.

We have found that without reading all business intercourse would be impossible. Without it man instantly becomes isolated and a savage; all past progress in physical freedom is of no further avail. But under the same conditions, the spiritual unity, through which man grows in spiritual freedom, is instantly broken; and man is at once isolated, and his life cannot be enlarged by the spirit of the race. By reading man adds to himself the present life of humanity; and not only this, but the life of the race through all time. He can infuse his life with the thoughts and aspirations of the witty and wise of the centuries. He can add to himself Plato and Paul,

Shakespeare and Emerson, and thus become exalted and magnified by the assimilation of each unto himself. Without reading, no vessel could cross the ocean to bring tea from China or coffee from Brazil; but neither could we have Homer or Gladstone, Gibbon or Bancroft. Thus reading preserves the spiritual unity of the race, as well as the industrial; and thereby makes it possible for man to be all that the race has become.

So each common-school branch might be shown to condition spiritual freedom in an analogous manner to its bearing on physical freedom. The common-school branches are said to be fundamental because they are obviously and absolutely essential to industrial life; but they might be so named for the reason that they absolutely condition progress in spiritual life. If there were no practical problem of life before us, these so-called instrumental branches must yet stand first in our curriculum, because they open the way for the mind to move out into the world of thought, and are best adapted to train its power. The common-school branches are as clearly culture studies for the child and youth as are the college studies for the mature; and this both in respect to knowledge and to discipline.

The final truth to be urged is, that if the teacher wield the common-school branches to the end of spiritual power he will more effectively secure the practical knowledge and training for the daily duties of life. For instance, suppose the teacher to be presenting the application of cubic measure to the measuring of wood, keeping only the spiritual good of the pupil in mind. The teacher knows that this external world which the pupil is to compass in thought is a world of form; and that the pupil masters that form by means of his mathematical imagination. He is to develop in him a new power and a new organ of thought by which he may grasp the world of form. To this end, having fixed the idea cube, he requires the pupil to image a row of eight cubes, and then beside this row three others. Then above these rows, another series; and so on, till four series are clearly imaged. The pupil's imagination is thus trained to impose its new instrument of knowing, the cube, on any concrete form; and is thus enabled to that extent to reduce the material world, in whatever form it may occur, to its own terms — becomes one with it. Let us now suppose that the teacher has so-called practical results in mind, and requires the pupil to follow the rule of multiplying length, breadth, and thickness together, and then dividing by 128. As to culture, the superiority of the first process is obvious; and as to practical value, it is equally so. If the pupil should remember his rule, he is limited to cord wood. The first process trains to a form of activity which will enable the pupil to throw anything into the cubic form; not only into feet, but into any other unit, as soon as the unit is known. This form of activity will reach into the practical world further than a hundred rules. A pupil thus trained may be dropped down into the practical world anywhere and he will fall on his feet every time. There has been a uniform complaint that pupils from the public schools could not measure wood, lumber, etc. This is because they have been trained simply to measure wood and lumber. If the spiritual necessity of the pupil had been kept in mind, the wood and lumber question would have been effectively disposed of.

Again, suppose a lesson in factoring, and one of the members 480. The mental freedom of the pupil requires that he be able to think things under the relation of product and factor. He must be given the power to do this, that he may enter into the world of thought about him. Suppose, with the given number, the teacher requires the pupil to make, on the board, a succession of divisions, according to the usual formula given for such work. This is the practical method; easily learned, and performed without effort. Instead of this, suppose the teacher, having regard for the faculty of the pupil, should require him to resolve the number mentally and instantly; thinking it into 48 tens, and while holding each of these composite factors to resolve them, saying, 2, 5, 2, 2, 2, 2, 3. This trains to a universal form of mental activity; and gives strength of thought by the intensity required. A teacher ought to be forbidden by law to require a pupil to solve such a problem as the above by the chalk process. Now it is easy, again, to see that the process here which is good for the mind of the pupil is the best for practical purposes. The pupil thus trained will solve five to one by the other process.

It is ever thus: the teacher who keeps an eye single to the spiritual good of the pupil will most effectively secure the practical ends of the subject. The two are not in opposition, but to secure both, the aim must rest in the higher. The teacher who levels his work to the merely practical will miss that and all else; but the teacher who seeks the kingdom of heaven will have all things else added. It will be worth while for the teacher who is interested in this thought, to reduce all of the common-school branches to means of spiritual life, and then note what a wonderful gain there has been in the interest of practical education. But this is asking much, for the whole of a professional education is involved in the problem of showing the life-giving function of the subjects we teach. To be conscious, in the teaching, how the means at hand is to reveal to the pupil his possibilities and give him a confidence and pride in his own worth; how it is to so inspire him with a longing for truth and righteousness that he can have no peace but in their pursuit; how it is to give his life definite current under a strong purpose, and a fullness and joy which lift above the turmoil of the lower world—to be conscious of these in teaching is the triumph of professional knowledge and skill.

In conclusion, then, the true aim of teaching is one with the true aim of life; and each lesson must be presented under the conscious purpose of making the most out of the life of the one taught. Every lesson in the common school should be made a means of liberal culture. The soul of the pupil has its own reasons for the activity stimulated and the knowledge acquired. We behold the rainbow and study its laws, and the reason is in the soul itself. The soul has its own reasons for knowing the history and structure of the earth, the laws of planetary motion, or the development of the human race "in its slow and toilsome march across the centuries toward freedom." The pupil is taught physiology, and stands in wonder at the miracle of organism before him. The knowing of this wonder is its own reason, and needs no excuse from practical hygienic laws. Tell the pupil who has touched the thought in the human body that physiology is studied to gain laws of dietetics and bathing, and he will tell you that it is a base insult; that he knows a spiritual good above the bodily welfare. There is no field of knowledge but what has immediate and direct relation to the soul. Emerson says something like this: "You cannot insult the sun, moon, and stars; they will serve him and him only who becomes a high-born candidate for truth." So the teacher must not insult the subjects of study by presenting them in any other way than as if to high-born candidates of truth.

METHOD IN TEACHING.

THE UNIVERSAL LAW.

The first of the universal factors, the purpose of teaching, has been considered to convince the teacher that in every lesson he should be conscious of the value of the experience produced in terms of the spiritual development of the child; that, for instance, in teaching a lesson in geography, the universal spiritual value of the lesson to the child should be the conscious guide in all that the teacher does; and that thus the utilitarian value of the subject will be more fully realized than if directly sought. In fact, the industrial end can furnish no guidance in the actual process of teaching. The universal value which the teacher is to feel, and by which he is to be guided, is in the experience produced, and not in something external and remote in time and application. The value is imminent in the experience itself; and is here and now and always to the pupil.

It is not sufficient for the teacher to hold vaguely and in general terms character as the end of the process; but the character-forming process must be concrete in the teacher's experience as he combines with the pupil in the learning act. Teachers quite readily assent to the doctrine of forming character as the end of teaching; and then go about their work as if they had been jesting in their theory. Intellectual assent to a doctrine is one thing; to make that doctrine real and subjective in one's life is quite another. The teacher must feel with his pupils the higher life into which they are being born under his touch; and not lose himself under the rubbish of school forms and technicalities, and then reappear and proclaim from the house-top that education is a power unto righteousness. The paralyzing contradiction between the mere assent of the intellect and the conviction of the heart must be removed so that our teaching life will be the embodiment and realization of what we proclaim in abstract theory. The argument in respect to the purpose of teaching was not made for the purpose of gaining assent to the doctrine of the supremacy of the spiritual aim in education, for we have been trained to accept that aim; but rather to illustrate the possibility and necessity of making that aim a guide and an inspiration in every concrete act of lesson hearing.

We come now to the discussion of the second universal element controlling the teaching process — the universal method in the process. Method is the way, the process, the movement, by which some end set up is realized. The teacher forms an ideal of the results to be attained in the life of the child, and then the process, or method, of realizing the ideal, claims his attention; *i.e.*, how the pupil unfolds his possibilities into actualities. The teacher takes him at a given point in growth and conducts him toward his highest destiny. The question is: How does the child grow? How does he move forward in the process of self-realization?

The Two Organic Phases of the Process. — These are the internal process of the mind's own free activity, and the external process of identification with external mind, or thought, as embodied in the objective world; for the external world is thought to the mind that thinks it. The mind grows through the process of uniting itself with mind embodied in things — the union of the subjective with the objective. As the internal process in the plant and in the animal require a correlative external process — as the external must be assimilated to the internal in physical life — so the internal process of mental life requires a correlative external process — the external objective thought and spirit of the world must be assimilated to the internal subjective spirit. The mind is free — has realized itself — to the extent to which it has identified itself with the thought of the world, and to the extent to which it has realized the possibilities of all its powers and faculties. The first is knowledge, or objective freedom; the second, discipline, or subjective freedom. The one looks inward: the other, outward. The internal process resulting in free realization through discipline is proportionate to the external process resulting in knowledge. In fact, the two are only obverse phases of the same truth; and the one resolves itself into the other. The broader and the more varied the spiritual horizon, the fuller and richer its subjective consciousness. This statement includes emotional life as well as intellectual. Subjectively considered, the emotions are free when all have been developed, and each is made pure and strong; and objectively, when they are rendered susceptible to the touch of the full range of objects known by the free intellect. And, too, the will, subjectively, must have full and constant control of the conscious life of the individual; and, as to environment, it must be in harmony with universal reason.

The onward movement of the life process must be stated in terms of the evolution of man's faculties — intellect (perception, memory, imagination, judgment, reason), sensibilities, and will. These faculties, as every true psychology shows, are not separate and distinct activities, but phases, or stages of the self in the ascending order toward spiritual freedom. For instance, perception involves every activity named after it; and each faculty after it involves the activity of all named before. They are not different and set over against each other as psychologies too often seem to hold; but each is a higher degree of freedom of the activity of the mind. The activity of every so-called faculty is at least implicit in every other faculty of the mind, whether we call that activity perception, memory, imagination, or thinking. We name the activity the one or the other of these to indicate the conscious element, and, therefore, the stage of freedom to which the mind has attained.

It is obvious that when man has only perceptive activity,

i.e., the perceptive element, the conscious one, he is confined in his spiritual activity to the presence of the material world — to the now and the here. He is limited by the external world, and has not yet become a limiter; he is conditioned, and cannot condition the world about him. He is enslaved by the sense-world, and lives only in the carnal mind. He is a sensuous being, and in danger of being sensual. As already observed, there is an increasing order of freedom in perception through the ascending order of the senses. Muscular perception requires the closest contact with the object perceived; touch, less so, yet there must be contact. In taste there is less of rigid contact with the object; the object itself is overcome and is in a state of dissolution. In perception through smell the individual is freed from contact with the object, perceiving that which lies beyond himself; while in hearing and sight perception extends over vast distances. This, by analogy, foreshadows the progress of the mind toward freedom in mastering the thought of the external world, and of the richer and fuller inner life correlative to the external freedom attained.

With all the freedom possible in mere perception, it is yet limited to the presence of the object perceived. Memory, in representing an object once present but not now so, gives the mind freedom in the real of past time. Man may have in mind all the world he has perceived without the presence of that world. While memory gives us the freedom of past time, imagination explores the the future. By it we produce ideas which have never been in past experience, and construct the world which lies beyond the reach of perception in space and in time. The narrow circle of sense perception is extended in space around the earth, to the solar system, and to the system of systems; and in time to the remotest past and into the boundless future. And by thinking, judging, reasoning, man finds the inner law and essence of things; finds the universe, "the law within the law"; finds behind all things self-activity, a soul, which is his own, and thus comes to the highest sense of spiritual freedom of which he is capable.

Or, put it in another form: The child at first is lost in the external, material world; is absorbed in it. It has only objective consciousness; it is not conscious of self; its own individuality and worth are not defined to it. This is the phase of pure perception. Then it begins to analyze, to dissect, to compare and contrast — to think, to reflect — and awakens to the consciousness that he is other than the thing he thinks. He finds relations and laws in a world other than himself; and that he has an individuality, a personality of his own; that he, too, is a center of force — plans, purposes, and executes; and that he has an inextinguishable hope for some good not yet attained. Finally, he discerns behind this world which stands over against him a self-conscious activity like himself — which is himself; finds himself in everything. The circle is now complete. At first he was at one with the external world, but unconscious of his own personality and worth; and at last he is one with the world; but is now conscious, through a course of reflection, of his own worth and his relation of unity with the world about him. In the second union his identity is not lost as it was in the first. The first unity is through the intuition of sense-perception; the second, through the intuition of reason. Between these two intuitions comes the exercise of memorizing, imagining, and judging, by which the separation is made and the condition for unity prepared.

The Two Factors in the Process. — These two foregoing organic phases of the process are so interfused that the discussion of either will involve and exhibit the other. They are related as cause and effect, since man realizes himself through phases of growth conditioned on the degree of unity realized between the self and the world beyond the self. Thus the universal problem of method is, how the learning mind identifies itself with the objective world to the end of growth, — how the subjective becomes one with the objective, in the process called knowledge. It ultimately resolves itself into a question of the nature of knowledge — knowledge as an organic process through the interaction of subject and object. The process called method in teaching is the product of two coördinate factors — the mind learning and the thing to be learned. Method is a form of mental action, — a form as much determined by the objective world as by the subjective. Without either, mental life would be impossible; therefore, both are essential and coördinate. In general, the problem of teaching is the same as the problem in philosophy — the relation of the subjective to the objective. To make this problem strictly professional, the relation considered must be viewed in its bearing on the teaching process. Philosophy is the most immediate of all studies to the problem of teaching.

It is a common thought that when a teacher is studying psychology he is necessarily pursuing a professional line of investigation; and that when zoölogy, for instance, is considered, the teacher has abandoned professional for academic ground. Zoölogy, physiology, arithmetic, grammar, etc., are, in their own nature, as strictly professional as psychology. None of them are professional unless viewed in relation to the teaching process; and the teaching process cannot be studied apart from the so-called academic studies.

The learning mind studies animals, and makes for itself the science of zoölogy. The mind here is one term in the process; animals is the other. Zoölogy is the mental formula for the animal kingdom. It exists only in the mind that thinks the animal kingdom; and we call that in the mind zoölogy when the subjective relations conform to the objective relations among the animals. Zoölogy names an organic body of knowledge; and this looks inward to the subjective form of thought as much as outward to the objective relations among animals. Zoölogy is in the mind as well as in the animal. In fact, on second thought, does it not seem more closely identified with the learning mind than with the animals learned? for zoölogy exists nowhere except in the mind that thinks animals after a given mode. It is of the mind; is mind. It requires no strained effort to conceive zoölogy as a form of mental activity in relation to the animal world. What is this form of activity, is the problem of method in teaching the animal kingdom.

The science called physiology is a mental thing, while the human body of which it treats is material. The relations in the mind corresponding to the relations in the body constitute the science of physiology. Physiology is the mind's form of activity in tracing the thought in the organism of the human body. When physiology is studied for the sake of this form of activity the study becomes professional. The physician studies the laws of organic action in the body that he may administer unto its welfare ; while the teacher desires to know how the mind forms the science of physiology in order that he may administer to the welfare of the mind studying. ✕

All the subjects of study, as arithmetic, grammar, geography, etc., name forms of mental life in relation to given subject-matter. And logic, the generalization of all the objective sciences, is the universal form of mental action in unity with the objective world ; and, therefore, more immediate to the problem of method than is psychology.

It has been well said that, "the law in the mind and the fact in the thing determine the method." The mind thinks sentences, plants, the earth ; and how it thinks in each case is determined by the laws of mind activity on the one hand, and by the nature of each object considered on the other. The nature of the earth has something to say as to how it shall be thought. The unity of the two factors in a mode of thought, in this case, is called grammar, botany, geography. Could anything be a more direct and legitimate object of pedagogical study than these academic branches when viewed as to the mode of thought exhibited?

Let it be noted that professional study is something more than a separate study of each of the two factors in the learning process. We often hear of the study of mind and the study of subjects as being correlative parts in a teacher's preparation; and the one is called educational psychology, and the other the professional study of the subject. But, to become professional, this quality must be given the form of unity in the process of mind growth. Educational psychology concerns itself with the method of the mind's growth in the subjects of study; and the professional study of subjects resolves them into the mind processes which they are fitted to stimulate and nourish. On the one hand the method of the mind's growth is pushed out into its exercise ground of objective mind in the form of subjects; while on the other, the subjects are resolved into educative mental processes. Thus the teacher of psychology and the teacher of the other subjects meet; and it is difficult to discriminate one from the other. The teacher of educational psychology must know the field of the mind's activity — that which it is to assimilate unto itself in the process of growth — before he can trace the process of growth; and the teacher of subjects must know the laws of mind which constitute the subjects before he can formulate their educational value in the process of the mind's assimilating them. Thus it appears that neither psychology nor the so-called academic subjects are in their own nature professional ; but both become so when viewed as a factor in determining the process of learning, and, therefore, of teaching. The teacher must think the mind to be taught into unity with the subject by which it is taught ; or, the subject to be taught into unity with the mind to which it is taught.

It is interesting and instructive to note what disposition professional schools have made of the two factors in the teaching process. The two parts in the teacher's preparation — psychology and the academic studies — have been recognized ; but not recognized as factors of the process. Psychology was taught as high-school psychology ; and the academic subjects were taught to give the teacher more knowledge of them than his pupils possessed ; but of the same kind. Aside from these, and constituting the strictly professional part of the work, the external process of instruction in the form of devices was considered, along with school organization and management. The study of external machinery had first professional recognition. Then we began to hear of educational psychology, and applied psychology ; suggesting at least a vague feeling that there must be a difference between pure psychology and the teacher's view of psychology.

At this stage of professional development in the normal school, the academic subjects were held not to be professional, and were taught only to enable the teacher to secure license. The teacher posted in them might well omit them in his professional investigation. The bulk of the work, however, was in these branches ; and the normal school was a high school with a professional attachment of psychology, with manipulation of school machinery. Presidents of normal schools deplore the humiliating necessity of having the common branches in the course, and wish for the time when they can be lopped off, making their schools in fact what they are in name — professional. But these schools must always teach the academic studies; not, however, as academic studies, but as educational instruments. The teacher must not only know the subjects as such, as a high-school pupil knows them, but must have that reflective knowledge of them which results from the analysis of his processes as he constructs those subjects. To discard this intimate knowledge of the concrete process of teaching, which only a most searching analysis of the subject can yield, for the history and philosophy of education and general method — method aside from particular subject-matter — is to assume that the teacher, in his preparation, reverses the accepted theory of education, and proceeds from the general and abstract to the particular and concrete. It is in accordance with the law of all learning for the teacher to trace the concrete process of learning and teaching in the particular subjects, before making his broader generalizations; such as required by the history and philosophy of education and the general laws of method.

It would be risking much indeed to equip the student with educational theory in the abstract and expect him to reduce his theory to the concrete working point in each of the subjects he is to teach. Nothing is a more common characteristic of the teacher than the fact that he has two professional lives, the one practical and the other theoretical; and the one having no relation to the other. This results from an effort to learn the profession by standing aloof from the actual educative process as produced by the subjects of study, and resting the case in the literature of the profession. Such teachers give fair talk with absurd practice. If they had risen from an actual experience of the educative process, as each of the subjects is peculiarly adapted to produce it, to a full realization of the best which history and philosophy of education reveal, the duality in the teacher's life would be reduced to unity. The philosophy of education is a vague abstraction, and general method only a formula for routine, unless grounded in the nature of education and its processes, which can only come by thinking the mind to be taught into the unity of the subject by which it is taught. Concrete, conscious experience must constitute the material of generalization — the material for the philosophy and methodology of the process. For such a purpose the academic studies must still appear in the normal-school course. We must not discard them for the sake of seeming professional. Because the academic school puts the student into these subjects for the purpose of liberal culture, the normal school need not be prevented from putting its students into the same subjects in order to reduce those subjects to educational instruments. The subject of grammar is taught in the public school for whatever end culture may require; in the normal school it is reduced to a conscious educational instrument. To this end its innermost constitution is explored, and all its processes traced out; their educational value ascertained, and the means of stimulating the processes fixed upon. All this must be done in the grammar; not out of it. The solution of the problem of a strictly professional school, therefore, does not come by the simple process of exclusion, but by the organic process of inclusion.

Method is the process of unity between the subjective and the objective; and this unity cannot be found if either factor of the process be omitted. But, to solve the problem of method, it must be shown how these two factors unite in the process of learning. This requires a statement of the *ground* and the *law* of their union.

The Ultimate Ground of Unity.—At first it seems absurd to speak of the mind identifying itself with the object; as, the tree, the earth, the sky, the state. These seem so utterly different from myself that I can never become one with them. The world about me seems to oppose me; to exclude me. Subject and object oppose each other; they are mutually exclusive. How can I ever become one with the steam engine which I am to think; with the Greek statue; the English Parliament; the solar system! Yet if I cannot, in some sense, become one with these objects, I cannot think them. To think an object is to reduce it to unity with the mind.

The materialist solves the problem of unity by reducing mind to a material principle; the idealist, by reducing the external world to an ideal principle of mind. In materialism, the subjective disappears in the external, material world; in idealism, the external vanishes in the subjective. The truth probably lies between; and the two worlds find their unity in reason, or thought, the essence both of the thinking mind and the world to be thought. The external world is thought in manifestation; and this thought is the common element in which the learning mind identifies itself with the object to be learned. On no other supposition can we think the external world. The mind cannot think something foreign to itself; something with which it holds no common element. Thought cannot stir itself, and language betrays the fact, except in the truth that there is a common element between the subjective mind and the objective world.

On the lowest plane of thought, that of sense-perception, and the one in which the difference between subject and object is most striking, we unconsciously assume a community of life between the self and the object; as shown by the language of sense-perception. When I say that the orange is sour, I think I speak of some objective truth in the orange; and I do. A second thought convinces me that the word *sour* names a subjective sensation. What I really mean by the word *sour* is the state of the self. I am in a state called *sour*; yet I cannot get rid of the consciousness that there is something in the orange named by the word *sour*. To speak of the bell as shrill is to speak in terms of subjective sensation, although it is the purpose to speak of an objective truth. If the orange and the bell could speak out of their own nature they might deny having the qualities which we assume correspond to our sensations; but we cannot rid ourselves of the consciousness that there is here a true unity between subject and object.

Again, if I affirm that this stone is heavy, I think I am speaking true to the fact in the stone; yet a moment's reflection convinces me that I am primarily speaking of my muscular tension. The giant, lifting it, would affirm in good faith that the stone is light. The difference between the weight of two objects can be asserted only in terms of muscular tension; and yet I cannot convince myself that the difference in my two tensions has not a unity with the difference in the two objects.

The difference between two objects, thought to be objective, is in neither of them. This one is red and that blue; in which is the difference? There is a change in the sensation of the optic nerve from red to blue. This change in experience is subjective; yet it is believed that there is a corresponding external change, called difference, with which it is in unity. One may say that this pinhead is large, believing that the truth he speaks is wholly objective. But he has only to change the standard of comparison, say to a mountain, to convince himself that the same pin-head is extremely small. Are not the large and the small in the mind, therefore, and not in the object as affirmed by the observer? Yes; and yet we cannot disbelieve their objective reality. Without reflection, the doubt of the external reality could not arise; on first reflection their subjective reality takes the place of the objective; on second reflection it is found that the consciousness of their reality cannot be displaced.

"To a Transcendentalist, Matter has an existence, but only as a Phenomenon ; were we not there, neither would it be there; it is a mere Relation, or rather the result of a Relation between our living Souls and the great First Cause ; and depends for its apparent qualities on our bodily and mental organs ; having itself no intrinsic qualities ; being, in the common sense of that word, Nothing. The tree is green and hard, not of its own natural virtue, but simply because my eye and my hand are fashioned so as to discern such and such appearances under such and such conditions. Nay, as an Idealist might say, even on the most popular grounds, must it not be so? Being a sentient Being, with eyes a little different, with fingers ten times harder than mine; and to him that Thing which I call Tree shall be yellow and soft, as truly as to me it is green and hard. Form his Nervous structure in all points the reverse of mine, and this same Tree shall not be combustible or heat-producing, but dissoluble and cold-producing, not high and convex, but deep and concave; shall simply have all properties exactly the reverse of those I attribute to it. There is, in fact, says Fichte, no Tree there ; but only a Manifestation of power from something which is not I. The same is true of material Nature at large, of the whole material Universe, with all its movements, figures, accidents, and qualities ; all are Impressions produced on me by something different from me." Thus again, when we are conscious that we speak of the objective a little reflection proves that our words refer to the subjective. And further reflection shows that the reality of the objective cannot be denied. Carlyle further suggests that we do not plunge over precipices and run ourselves through with swords by way of recreation, these being only phantasms and spectra, and therefore of no consequence. More than this; we must assume some common relation between the objective and the subjective in order to think the objective. To think an object is to bring it into terms of unity with the thinker.

We assume that our idea of number is derived from things; but Pythagoras affirms that things are based on number. The theorem that the square of the hypotenuse is equal to the sum of the square of the other two sides of a right-angled triangle is true according to subjective laws of thought; and, too, it may be shown to be true as an objective reality. It is said by some one that mathematics is based on the assumption that what is ideally true is really, externally true.

The bridge is built according to laws of thought; the external reality of these laws is tested in the train's passing over in safety. All of the complicated lines and figures drawn in geometry by the subjective laws of thought may be traced in actual relations in the external world. The transformation of an equation in algebra is an external transformation in the concrete world.

The student in physics feels at first that he treads the firm earth of objective reality, yet soon he is forced to feel that it has an ideal and subjective foundation. The molecule of which he has so much to say, is a mental necessity; a creation of the imagination. He learns that a body set in motion moves in a straight line and forever. A moment's reflection convinces him that this phenomenon has not taken place and cannot take place, except in the subjective laws of thought. Says Huxley: "Matter and Force are, as we know them, mere names for certain forms of consciousness." But his good faith in the reality of matter and force, and that in them were laws akin to his own mind, was the indispensable condition to the prosecution of his scientific labors. "If we trace all our conceptions on the nature of Force to their fountain head, we shall find that they are formed on our own consciousness of Living Effort — of that force which has its source in our own vitality, and of that kind of it which can be called forth at the bidding of the Will." [1] The reality of the external material force can no more be questioned than can the internal force called will. If these two forces are wholly distinct and incommensurable, all thought of the forces in the world is a dream and a delusion. The mind's feeling of unity with the forces of the world cannot be dispelled; and on this feeling it proceeds in good faith to explain the nature of force and formulate its laws.

In the realm of organic nature, unity is more clearly implied. Darwin quite uniformly speaks of adaptation, design, mental purpose, in describing the truth in the objective world. These words name mental relations in the concrete world which are in unity with mental relations in the subjective world. The plant and the animal

[1] Argyll in the Reign of Law.

are reduced to terms of mind; then the student feels to be one with them. They have become a part of his mind; his mind has taken on the form of thought in the plant and the animal. To think the animal is to retrace the thought embodied in it; and this assumes a common term between the mind and the animal. If there is no thought in the human body, we could not think it. This thought in it is of the nature of our own thought; and hence the unity which may be established between our own mind and it.

In general, the laws of our thinking and the laws of being are one. This is well illustrated in the history of the categories. Aristotle set forth the relations under which an object exists. These relations we know as the categories of being; purpose and means; cause and effect; time and place; whole and part; substance and attribute; and likeness and difference. Any object exists only by virtue of these relations. The tree cannot exist without existing in the relation of space and time, whole and part, cause and effect, etc. Kant affirms that these categories are the subjective laws of thought; that these are the forms by which the mind thinks the objective world; it grasps objects under these relations because these are its innate modes of activity. Hegel would say that both are correct; that the laws of thinking and being are one. On this assumption only can the mind of the learner identify itself with the object to be learned.

A splendid illustration of this doctrine of unity between the thinking mind and the object thought is Spencer's System of Philosophy, in which he shows that the law by which all things come into being in the world is the same law by which the mind thinks the world of being. From this reference the reader can readily supply illustrations of the parallel between psychological laws and the laws of objective existence.

In this ground of unity between the self and the objective world is discovered the laws of motive in learning, in obedience to which means in teaching must be wielded. We have seen that the fundamental fact of human spirit is a striving of its own impulse to realize itself; and to this end it craves to make its own the world of thought which lies beyond it. Man instinctively feels that, beyond his own life in the world about him, there is a life akin to his own; which must flow into his own to satisfy his longing for more life. He feels that everything is the manifestation of a universal life of which his own life is a part; and that to realize his possibilities he must participate in that universal life. This is the meaning of the proverbial curiosity of the child. It strives unceasingly, by means of all the senses, to get into the life of the object. A blind impulse urges it to a good it knows not of, — a good through the object which it strives to make its own. To know is its own reward; because in knowing there is immediate consciousness of realizing the self in the object; of rising to the higher self, to the life and thought in the object. All means are based on this innate tendency of the mind to know the external world. The highest test of a teacher's skill in the use of means is whether he causes the pupil to find his life in the object; to feel that some craving of the soul is gratified and its growth nourished.

This feeling of unity with the subject under discussion is what is known as interest, the most pervasive idea in the art of teaching. The word interest (*inter* and *esse*) means to be between. When a pupil feels that the subject before him stands as a means between his present, real self and his future, ideal self, he is interested in that subject. A teacher who can truly interest pupils in the subject has attained maximum skill in the use of means. There is a popular notion of interest, however, which does not fall under this description; it is interest for the sake of interest, or amusement. The interest must be in the thing studied and not in some external contrivance to persuade the pupil to endure the subject being taught. A pupil may be induced to strive to excel in grammar through the unworthy motive of emulation, without being interested because he finds his life in the subject. It is one thing to interest a pupil in his *per cents*, but another thing to interest him in his geography. The greatest show of interest in school work is not a guarantee of interest in the search for knowledge. The teacher may have invented extraneous sources of attraction to balance a failure to stimulate by the touch of life in the subject. Thus it follows that where there is a high degree of interest awakened by external devices we may suspect the teaching to be dead and formal.

To hold *per cents*, or like means, over pupils as an inducement or a threat is not only unnecessary, but positively vicious; for unless the pupil finds gratification in the subject itself he will form no tendency to future study; he may even form an aversion to it. The teacher guides the pupil's study but a short time; but during that time he should give the pupil a life-long tendency to seek truth. There is no greater evil in education than that of deadening the natural appetite for knowledge; and this is done by urging through the course on external pressure. At the end pupils give a sigh of relief, rather than feel a restless longing for truth and righteousness.

Even after proper means have been selected, all diligence must be used to keep them from intercepting the pupil's thought and prevent it from going direct to the object. A map and globe are good things; but a pupil may never see beyond them to the earth. Diagramming a sentence may, occasionally, be a convenient means; but how often is it used so that the pupil studies the diagram and not the sentence! Whatever the aids used in picturing a battle, they must be so used that the pupil will be a direct observer and will feel without hindrance the strife and heroism. Not only should he not be thinking on the words of the text, but the map of the battlefield must disappear for the real field with its woods, hills, ravines, and surging armies. The aids of text and cuts in physiology must disappear, leaving the mind in free contact with the organ studied. The distinction between good teaching and bad is sharply drawn; in one the means are so used as to bring the mind into vital touch with the thought in the object; in the other, they are so used as to intercept the free activity on the object.

The child not only craves to find its life as already embodied in things, but is moved to express its life in external forms. This is the obverse side of the preceding truth; but it is the same craving for unity with objective being. He is an originator, a self-active being, and cannot rest till he makes his thought and purpose valid in the external world. He rejoices at every opportunity to manifest his power. Difficulties challenge him to greater effort. He is happiest in work when his powers, without useless effort, are engaged to their full capacity. Work must neither be too difficult nor too easy; one is as fatal to interest as the other. The teacher often destroys interest by assigning matter so difficult, or in such an obscure way, as to cause useless and vexing effort. The pupil desires his labor to bear fruit; and while we talk of activity for the sake of the discipline, the pupil will still demand a satisfaction in the form of objective truth. On the other hand, the teacher will as often fail to secure interest by assigning work unworthy of his powers, or by giving too much assistance. The lesson is often questioned into little bits, when it would stimulate a higher degree of self-activity for the pupil to work on the matter as a whole and discuss it without continual prompting. Independent and original research is said to be characteristic of university work; but is not this the true principle for all school work? for by this means the teacher respects the pupil's freedom and self-activity. In the advanced work the pupil is given a longer period of freedom; but the principle is the same. A child may reach the end of his investigation of a butterfly in ten minutes; but it is independent and original research to all intents and purposes. A pupil in the high school can sometimes work with profit for two or three days on an historical problem, books and references having been supplied. His self-activity is thus challenged, and he will acquire more strength than by depending on the teacher to lead his thought through the details by countless questions. But in whatever way it is done the teacher must respect the self-activity of the pupil, to the end that he be both interested and made capable of independent work — to the end that the teacher become useless to him as soon as possible.

Thus while the teacher devises means in a given act of teaching, on discerning what the mental steps are in learning the object, he must recognize and respect, as a universal condition of all means, the natural impulse of the pupil to do and to know; and the power of the subject, when properly adjusted, to gratify the impulse.

The Ultimate Law of Unity. — The mind of the learner is confronted with the objective world; with this he is to identify himself. The possibility of so doing rests on a community of nature between the two. The assumption is that both the external and the internal worlds are worlds of thought, of reason. The external world is idea, or thought, manifested. The external world is only the larger self of the individual. He is one with it to the extent to which he masters its thought. The thought in one is the thought in the other. We come now to suggest something of the process by which this is done — the process of method in teaching. First in general outline, then in specific phases.

Man first meets the objective world in the form of concrete individual objects present to the senses. At this point there seems the widest gulf between the mind and the object. That is, it seems so to the reflective mind. To the child it is otherwise; for it loses itself in the material world. But to us, the gulf between mind and matter seems impassable. And indeed it is so, on the material plane. The material, sensuous thing must be penetrated to the idea in it.

Every individual has its reality in a universal truth. The individual waves of the sea arise out of the universal sea. There must be universal being back of every individual existence; and this universal being is not a material thing. It cannot be found by observation. It is idea, thought, reason.

The individual sewing machine has, as its reality, the universal idea sewing machine. The idea sewing machine can produce infinitely individual sewing machines. Destroy all the individuals, and the idea will cause them to reappear; showing that the idea is the abiding reality, and not the individuals. The reality of a thing never appears to the senses; but the sense-individual embodies an idea, a mental something, to which the mind must penetrate in learning it. In my walk I come to the Presbyterian church, and feel that I have before me a substantial reality. Yet remove the idea of its architect, and it is no more than a material substance. Back of the architect's idea yet, it has its being in the religious idea of the Presbyterians of this city. Their thought created it, and supports it. But the Presbyterians of this city are only a portion of Presbyterianism. Without Presbyterianism there could be no Presbyterians of this city. So that this church has its reality in Presbyterianism in general. Presbyterianism in general is only a phase of Protestantism. Without Protestantism there could be no Presbyterianism; without Presbyterianism, no Presbyterianism of this city. Hence this church has its reality in Protestantism. Again, Protestantism is a phase of Christianity. No Christianity, no Protestantism; no Protestantism, no Presbyterianism; no Presbyterianism, no Presbyterianism in this city. This church, therefore, has its reality in Christianity. Christianity is grounded in the universal religion of the human heart. This is the ultimate reality of this church. Without it the spire would never have pointed heavenward. It is one of the myriads of waves tossed out of the sea of religious spirit. The mind, in becoming unified with this church, must not only identify itself with the architect's idea, but must see it as the embodiment of the religious spirit and history of the world. The mind of the learner in identifying itself with this church looks through the individual manifestation to the mind out of which it arose.

The learner will first meet John Brown's Raid as an individual fact, having definite time and place. This Raid had its being in the vigorous spirit of freedom arising in behalf of the slave. The history of the anti-slavery sentiment was in that single act. The anti-slavery spirit was a phase of the spirit of freedom born in the American Revolution. Concord and Lexington, Valley Forge and Yorktown were all in John Brown's Raid; they arose out of the same universal sentiment. The history of Europe in its struggle for religious and political liberty conditioned this Raid; even Magna Charta and the Bill of Rights are, only antecedent forms of it. The universal spirit of Christianity, proclaiming the brotherhood of man, is the reality of the event under consideration. To read this event aright one must read the history of the world into it. Any event in history arises out of some idea, or sentiment, which multiplies itself in countless forms. To learn an event, therefore, is to come in touch with the universal idea on which the event rests. In this way all events in history become united; they are all rooted in some fundamental, universal phase of human life. To become one with this life is to learn history. Then the mind has come into unity with the individual object studied. While the object remained a mere individual, the unity could not be made. To this end the mind must feel its way to a self-active, self-conscious power like its own.

Every individual object reflects the universe. To know an object completely is to see the universe in it; and this includes the self. "The curtain beside me, were my ear so fine, would whisper of mines and miners, and looms and fields of mulberry, and of logwood cutters and camp-fires in far-away lands. All these are related to it as it hangs; and if I knew it well I might feel the draught of Uranus in its folds." Yes, and if we knew it well we could perceive in it, too, the thought of humanity. The physical and spiritual forces of the world resolve themselves into the curtain.

The student first grasps the Amazon River as an individual object — gives it location, form, and feature. He sees it as a magnificent panorama of landscape. Then he proceeds to find the reality of the Amazon in the universe lying beyond it. He sees the form and contour of South America in the river. The winds and the rains form it. The Atlantic Ocean is its fountain. The revolution and the rotation of the earth help condition it. The sun is over it, determining, with other conditions, where it shall be and that it shall be the largest river in the world. The moon and stars are in its current; and if we knew it well we could hear Uranus in the flow of its waters. The reality of the Amazon is in the cosmic forces of the universe; and if the universe is a universe of law and reason, this river must have its origin in that law, or reason. All physical phenomena resolve themselves into physical forces; and all physical forces resolve themselves into the unity of a single force. And force can only be known in terms of will; hence we are compelled to assume an infinite will as the origin of all things. When we reach this self-conscious purpose which creates and supports the object, we recognize ourselves in it — have made the unity sought.

The poet best illustrates the unity of the self with the individual object through the perception of the universal truth embodied in the object. Goethe says that the poet calls the individual object to its universal consecration. He finds in it a universal law of spiritual life; and therefore of my life. He reads behind the phenomena of the physical world the spiritual world on which it rests. Natural history, says Emerson, is for the purpose of supernatural history. The physical world serves us best only when it reveals the spiritual world. To the poet every individual object reveals a spiritual law; and when I have seen that law, I have found myself. Bryant, in beholding the water-fowl with the physical eye, beheld with the spiritual eye the guidance of human life by Divine Providence. He felt his own life and the water-fowl's to be one. This was a much closer identification than could have been made by an ordinary zoölogical study. The poet is one who adjusts "his inward eye to the proper focus with the outward organ." Should not the pupil make this adjustment with every object he studies? As we have seen, in the study of the pyramid, the pupil should make the object a law of spiritual life unto himself; his own being must be reflected in it. This is the point at which the pupil reaches inspiration and ecstasy in learning; because at this point he realizes something of his ideal self.

Thus the most universal law of method, in unifying the self with the objective world, appears to be this: the mind first fixes itself on the individual object by means of the senses, and then moves outward till the spiritual sense discerns the universal truth in which it has its ultimate being, returning with the universal truth to the individual — from the individual to the universal, and back to the individual. We sometimes say that we pass from the individual to the general; but the mind really passes from the individual to the individual, through the general, or universal. The individual from which the mind starts is not the same as that to which it returns; for it finally returns with the truth of the universe in the individual. We grasp the individual first by means of the intuition of the senses; and last by the intuition of the reason. Between these two the judgment seizes the general as a means of reaching the universal. The universal law of method in learning may be shown by the following diagram, representing the subjective and the objective world confronting each other : —

Subjective $\begin{cases} \text{Reason, Intuition.} \\ \text{Judgment.} \\ \text{Perception (}^{\text{inner and}}_{\text{outer}}\text{).} \end{cases}$ $\begin{matrix} \text{Universal.} \\ \text{General.} \\ \text{Individual.} \end{matrix}\Big\}$ Objective

Thus the mind first grasps the individual object by means of perception or the sensuous imagination. It becomes aware of the world of the senses. The individual does not exist in its isolation; but is a center of forces which reach beyond it — forces circling wider and wider until the ultimate force of the universe is reached. This increasing width and power of relations which determine the individual must be grasped by the progressive unfolding of the faculties of the understanding and the reason. The individual object is to be given deeper and still deeper significance as rapidly as the unfolding powers of the mind permit. The mind, in its unfolding order in any process of thought, or in its order of development, parallels the relations of the individual in the objective world. The individual object has, first, its isolating, its individualizing, attributes; second, relations connecting it with its environment; and, third, the ultimate conditions of its existence. Through perception the mind seizes the isolating, individualizing attributes; through the understanding, the relations to the world of objects about it; and through reason, the ultimate conditions of its being. Dr. Harris thus speaks of these as phases of knowing: —

"The first stage of knowing concentrates its attention upon the object, the second upon its relations, and the third on the necessary and infinite condition of its existence. The first stage of knowing belongs to the surface of experience, and is very shallow. It regards things as isolated and independent of each other. The second stage of experience is much deeper, and takes note of the essential dependence of things. They are seen to exist only in relation to others upon which they depend. This second stage of experience discovers unity and unites in discovering dependence of one upon another. The third stage of experience discovers independence and self-relation underlying all dependence and relativity. The infinite, or the self-related, underlies the finite and relative, or dependent."

The simple, practical truth to be held is this: The pupil first seizes the object as an isolated thing, and then thinks into it, as rapidly as his knowledge and unfolding powers permit, progressively wider, and therefore deeper and more essential, relations until the ultimate ground of its being is reached. In this the pupil does not lose sight of the individual. We sometimes speak as if, in the process of knowledge, the mind soared away from the individual into the upper air of generalizations and abstractions. Generalizations and abstractions mean nothing unless concreted in the individual. Hypotheses and major premises must justify themselves in the court of concrete reality. While the individual points outward to the general, the general gravitates to the individual. The mind, in learning, must rise from the individual to the merely general, and to the universal; but it also must descend from the universal and general to the individual.

If the foregoing is the fundamental law of learning, it follows that the fundamental defect in teaching is that of presenting the object as a merely isolated individual. Its content is not enriched by the multitude of relations which connect it with the universe; and therefore the mind is not required to put forth its full round of activities of thought, emotion, and volition. An event in history is a thing of time and place and picturable features. It is not made to throb with the life of the race. In teaching the form of the earth, it is left as an empty thing, requiring only, perhaps, some external proof. That form is not seen in the life of man on the earth; in his industries and his institutions. Its direct relation to light and heat on the globe is not usually required; much less its indirect relations to plant and animal life; and still less its more indirect and remote relations to civilization. Or, what is the same thing, civilization is not seen in it. The child is not made to think to what extent the form of the earth is in his own life. The form of the earth passes out into a multitude of relations, immediate and remote, direct and indirect, simple and complex; and to be known thoroughly must be seen in all these relations; and these relations must all be seen in it. The individual must thus always be made to appear in the general, and the general in the individual. This does not mean that all the relations must be grasped at the time the pupil learns the fact; but that these relations, in their progressive order of remoteness and generality, should be grasped as rapidly as the unfolding knowledge and powers of the pupil permit. This suggests the principle on which a graded course of study must be formed.

A graded course of study is determined by the degree of generality which a given class of pupils can grasp. The fact of the earth's form and some of its immediate relations may be taught to a primary class. A circle of wider relations is fit subject-matter for an intermediate class; and the grammar grade can grasp still wider relations. Still more complex and comprehensive relations are adapted to the high-school pupil; and the college student would yet find enough to tax his powers to the utmost. A course of study is not made by introducing different branches of study for different grades; but by presenting higher and still higher phases of the same subject-matter. All subjects in the university have their roots in the primary school. The child enters school with something of psychology, astronomy, and politics. The course of study is but the progressive unfolding of the subject-matter given at the outset. It consists of related lines of thought running through from the first year of school to its close — the warp of the course; having equal degrees of generality in the lines set to be learned in the same stage of the pupil's development — the woof of the course. This would rearrange, somewhat, our present system. For instance, some phases of arithmetic are more general than some in algebra and in geometry. This means that some phases of arithmetic should be taught after some phases of algebra and geometry. Arithmetic should be pushed up, and algebra and geometry should be pulled down, till equal degrees of generality come at the same stage of the pupil's development. Geometry should extend all the way through school life.

The fundamental law of method suggests an important truth concerning the teacher's preparation. The teacher, in presenting any phase, should know its relation to the preceding and succeeding phases. The primary teacher, for instance, who presents an individual object and initiates the pupil's movement out into the widening circle of relations, will need to perceive all the relations, even out to the universal. He must see the end from the beginning. No primary teacher can move with a steady and assured progress who sees only relations to the extent of the ability of the class. And, also, the teacher of higher grades should know the relations upon which his work is conditioned. He must see the beginning from the end. Teachers and normal schools have too much faith in the direct preparation for doing a given grade of work. Specific methods may be of service, but they can never guide and inspire as do the ever widening relations of the subject and the profoundest laws of life in the student, — relations in the subject and in life which go far beyond what the teacher is immediately dealing with.

So far in the discussion of universal method, two points have been reached : —

1. Method is the movement by which the mind of the learner identifies itself with the thought and spirit of the world other than himself, and thus participates in the universal life of the world, which is his inheritance.

2. The fundamental law in the foregoing movement is that the mind, in the function of the senses, understanding, and reason, rises from the individual through the general to the universal, and descends from the universal through the general to the individual. On the lowest plane, by means of the intuition of the senses, the mind becomes aware of concrete objects in the sensuous world ; on the highest plane, by the intuition of the reason, the mind becomes aware of truth, beauty, and goodness as manifested in the concrete world. Between these two lie the processes of the understanding — abstraction, comparison, generalization, induction, and deduction — not an immediate seizing as with the other two, but by the conscious process with the relations among objects builds a kind of Jacob's ladder from the sensuous earth to the spiritual heavens.

SPECIFIC PHASES OF THE LAW.[1]

So far we have traced, in most general outline, the movement of the mind in learning the object under consideration. This process is now to be reduced to its specific phases and concrete working point in teaching.

In the thought movement above described, the individual is held in the grasp of two sets of relations: one which gives the object its distinct individuality, isolating it from every other object; another which connects the object with other objects. If we blot out all the differences between this table and all other tables, or between it and furniture, or trees, this table disappears. It cannot be a table without marks which separate it from other things. If, likewise, we take away all the attributes common to this table and all other tables, or common to furniture or trees, this table disappears. It cannot exist without common attributes. The object must have its own unity, and its unity with the universe. We cannot think an individual without putting into it a meaning broader than its own individuality.

This brings us to two attributes already mentioned; the individual and the universal; the first separating from, and the second connecting with, all other objects in the universe. Thus the individual object is grasped as an organic

[1] This chapter covers some of the ground treated in the second chapter of my Science of Discourse; and, when serving my purpose, I have used paragraphs from that discussion.

unit in itself; or as in unity with other individuals. This unity with other individuals is either through an organic relation with other individuals; or through a common nature, a common origin, with other individuals. But when an individual enters into organic relation with other individuals, a new individual is formed; thus leaving but one unity aside from the organic individual — the unity of a common nature with other individuals. For instance, John Smith has his own individual organic unity. He is also in unity with the world about him; and in two ways: in one way he is in unity with other persons because he is in organic relations with them — coöperating with them for a common good. In this way he helps to form a higher and a more complex individual organism; as, a school, a church, a state. In the other way, he is in unity with other persons through the common idea man; the idea in which all men have their origin.

Thus, the individual objects, ocean, lake, river, continent, island, mountain, etc., coöperate to form the organism, earth. All objects are thus held in the grasp of a unifying force. All things act and react on all things. "There is not a red Indian hunting by Lake Winnipic, can quarrel with his squaw, but the whole world must smart for it; will not the price of beaver rise? It is a mathematical fact that the casting a pebble from my hand alters the centre-of-gravity of the universe."

What are commonly known as individual objects act and react upon each other; coöperating in larger and still larger unities, which are themselves individuals, to some single result. Thus we have to deal only with the individual in *organic unity*, or in *class unity*.

The organic unity constituting the individual is through the coöperation of attributes and parts to the end of the individual; the class unity, as already suggested, is through the idea which gives origin to the individuals. The parts of the tree, root, trunk, and branches, coöperate to accomplish the purpose of the tree; thus making the tree an organic unit. But the tree has not only this unity in itself; it has unity with all other trees in the idea which originated them. The individuals forming the parts of the class unit do not coöperate for the good of the individuals or the class; but the parts of an individual, which are themselves as much individuals as are the parts of the class, do thus coöperate. This chair has parts and attributes bound into unity through the end which the chair has to serve; but this chair does not coöperate with other chairs to form the class chair. The individual chairs forming the class have their unity in the single idea originating all chairs.

The parts of the organic individual are bound together in space and time through interdependence; the parts of the class are bound together in identity of nature. In both cases there are parts; but in the first, the unity is because of differences; in the second, because of likenesses. There could be no organic unity among the parts of the sewing machine if the parts were the same; since each part in an organism has a different function. There could be no unity in the class sewing machine except through identity of idea which produces each individual, forming a part of the class.

Note the fact that the parts of the organic unit and of the class unit are not different in themselves; but that the difference lies in their relation to each other. The parts of a class become parts of an individual as soon as these parts begin to coöperate — assume interdependencies to achieve some good for the whole of which they are parts. The class of people called teachers organize and thus become an individual — an organization. Certain objects, when thought of as to their common nature, are called planets; but thinking of the same individuals in organic relation, they are called the solar system. When speaking of men, we think of individuals forming a class, because we think of them as having a common origin; but we must also think of them as organized for the good of each and all. Englishmen have a common blood, a common genesis. In this they have their class unity, and as such are treated by the ethnologist. But the historian treats them as one organized life — organized into industrial, civil, and cultural institutions. Or, to turn the illustration about, the organic earth has parts, and these parts may be viewed in classes; as, rivers, mountains, etc. Thus the parts of an organic unit may be thought into classes, and the parts of a class into an organic unit.

Let it be observed that the idea which originates the individuals of a class is infinite as to the number it may produce. There is no limit, so far as the idea is concerned, to the number of reapers the idea reaper can produce. So that a class cannot be thought as bounded in time or space. The moment this is done, the individual group, assembly, congregation, or such, is formed. Thus the individual must be thought as having its unity in space and time; while the class is not thus defined. A class may be bounded, but this is not essential to the thought of the class, while it is to the individual. Superficially, to give anything individuality in thought is to impose on it space and time boundaries.

Individuals are of increasing complexity from the simple atom to the universe. We are accustomed to suppose that the thinking of classes is a higher form of mental activity than that required in thinking individuals. This would be true were the individual always the simpler individual. But individuals rise into complexity until the highest individual, the universe, includes within it all classes. To describe a pencil or narrate a journey requires an elementary form of activity; but to describe the earth as an organism affecting the development of the human race, or to narrate the development of human life on the earth, requires a different order of thinking.

Hence, from the view taken of the object, there are two processes of teaching: one process presenting the individual in itself, as Chicago, the Brooklyn Bridge, that tree, this mental act; the other process presenting the individual as to its unity of idea with other individuals, giving rise to the class — general notion — concept; as, city, friendship, government. It is practical guidance for the teacher to know that, whatever the subject to be taught, the objects to be presented are of these two kinds. In geography, it is the earth, or some individual part of it, as, Rocky Mountains, Gulf Stream, London; or classes of parts, as, rivers, winds, continents. In history, it is this or that individual event, or classes of events; or the organic life of the people taken in unity. In arithmetic, it is this or that individual relation, as, five-sixths divided by two; or particular relations generalized into a law — the truth concerning each individual relation which makes possible the other relations. There will be an individual problem of carpeting a room; but the general law of carpeting rooms must be developed. And so through all topics to be taught; it is the individual viewed in its own inherent constitution; or in its unity of nature with other individuals. The latter view gives rise to what is known as the general object, general notion, class, or concept. The object under the first view is simply known as the individual.

We have thus descended one step from the universal law summed up on page 108. By that law the mind elevates the individual into its universal signification; it passes in a circle from the individual to the universal, and back to the individual, holding the universal and individual in unity. The method of doing so is by thinking the individual under its relations of organic and class unity. Obviously, the next problem is, how to think the individual and the general object.

THINKING THE INDIVIDUAL.

The Two Phases of the Process.— Each individual must be thought either as it exists in a fixed, a statical, form; or in a changing, a dynamical, form. These are not different individuals, for every object must exist in these two relations; but different ideas formed of the same individual, according as the mind views it under one or the other of these relations. The tree can be viewed as it exists at a given moment, with its parts and attributes coexisting; or in course of development from the seed to its present form — with consecutive attributes and parts. It requires both relations to fill out the idea tree. The mind may be viewed with its attributes and faculties as they exist at a given moment, or as changing in successive moments of time, — the mind fixed, with attributes and faculties coexisting, or the mind with its attributes and faculties manifested in successive moments of time. It requires both these relations to fill out the idea mind. But these individuals cannot be viewed in both these relations at the same time; and in the process of thought the mind makes of the actual individual two thought individuals. The tree or the mind may, in the same lesson, be presented in both phases of its existence; but there would be yet two distinct processes. The actual individual, however, is usually classed as either a fixed or a changing individual, according as the static or the dynamic relation is prominent. In fact, it is at first difficult to view some fixed individuals, as the earth, and some moving individuals, as a battle, or a process of digestion, in but one way. Yet a battle and digestion have parts that coexist. Besides, the successive parts are conceived as they exist in given moments.

The conception of a change in time is the result of the comparison of the individual as statical in two successive moments. While the object is changing, it still has co-existing attributes and parts; and these must be held in mind while the object is viewed as changing. There can be no conception of an individual as changing, without involving the conception of the individual as fixed. At this moment the growing orange consists of a given form, size, flavor, odor, and parts; without conceiving these as coexisting, it is impossible to think the next change it may undergo. An object cannot be perceived in the act of change. The change is inferred from a comparison of the object at a given moment with itself at a preceding or a succeeding moment. Hence the process of thinking the object as changing is conditioned on the process of thinking it as fixed. The former process brings the student nearer to the truth in the object; for it is the nature of things to change. Every object, in "fulfilling its own nature, passes out from its own nature." Thus, thinking an object as changing discloses the moving force which is its life and being.

The two ways of thinking the individual are determined by the fact that the mind thinks everything under the form of coexistence or of sequence — under forms of space and time. Or, it would amount to the same thing to say that the two ways of thinking the individual are determined by the nature of the object, which is, that it at the same time exists in space and endures in time. Even spiritual objects are figured under forms of space. One cannot think emotions without projecting them out in external form, side by side, in space. They are divided and set over against each other as are, in thought, the parts of a tree. The fact that the two ways of thinking the object, above set forth, are determined either by the nature of the thinking mind or of the object which the mind thinks, emphasizes once more the fact of unity between the thinker and the object which he thinks.

Individuals also differ as to the way in which they are first presented to the mind. One class is first known through the senses; the other, through consciousness. That particular tree is first known through the senses; that particular state of sadness is first known through consciousness. Thus we have material individuals and spiritual individuals. When presenting individuals the teacher will always be concerned with one or the other of these kinds. The pupil will be thinking his own mind or a mineral; Milton or a mountain; a poem or a pencil; the life of a people or the land on which they dwell, etc. Some objects, such as Gladstone or London, have a material and a spiritual side. London is organized life and not merely buildings and streets. In fact, every material object should be reduced back to its immaterial force, at least; if not to its spiritual content. A word, on one side, is a material thing; but it is the embodiment of an immaterial idea. A statue is a form of granite; but no study of it as a mere material thing would suffice. Its spiritual content must be reached. A rainbow is a physical phenomenon; but its physical analysis does not exhaust it, or reach the best it has for man. A lily is a physical organism; and, while it must be analyzed as such, the ear must be adjusted to its whisper of infinite truth and beauty. The individual material thing is the expression of a universal spiritual truth. The material world is the manifestation of the spiritual; and must be resolved into it. Of course we speak here of the poetic transformation of the material object. But such a process is only the penetration to its real meaning. When Lowell says, "With our faint hearts the mountain strives," he gives as substantial and undoubted an attribute of the mountain as the geographer could discover, and of infinitely more significance to the interests of man. Thus the material and the spiritual nature of objects mingle; and this fact must be observed in their treatment; the two worlds are organically related; and while every individual must be viewed as to how it is at a given moment and how it came to be what it is, it must be made to face both the material and the spiritual world.

The two teaching processes, presenting coexistent individuals and consecutive individuals, correspond to the two discourse processes presenting the same, called *description* and *narration*, whether presenting material or spiritual individuals. These names are appropriate to the teaching processes, so that we may speak of the process of teaching by description, and the process of teaching by narration.

Thinking the Individual as Fixed.

The individual is never simple; but is a unity of complex ideas. The problem is to cause the pupil to think the complex idea under the relation of unity.

First, the mind, by means of perception, becomes conscious of the individual as an object merely differentiated from other objects; then the judgment analyzes the object into its elements; and organizes the elements into the individual. The mere something of which the mind is first aware, becomes, through analysis and synthesis, a definite, organic individual — an individual organized about some central principle. The first step, that of seizing the object as an undifferentiated whole, is made without effort on the part of the pupil; but he must make a conscious effort in analyzing and synthesizing the elements. These two phases move hand in hand; as he analyzes he synthesizes, and as he synthesizes he further analyzes. The analysis keeps one pace ahead; but synthesis must organize as soon as each new element is found. Thus, while analysis precedes synthesis, the analysis of the object is not completed before the synthesis is begun.

The constituent elements into which the individual must be analyzed are *attributes* and *parts*. An individual cannot exist or be conceived without either. The distinction between attributes and parts is based on whether there is mutual exclusion. Attributes fuse — coincide; parts exclude each other. The length and breadth, the weight and strength, the cost and use of the Suspension Bridge coincide; the parts, as braces and ropes and beams, each excludes the other from its own place.

The perception that an object has parts is conditioned on the perception of its attributes; for a part must be distinguished from the whole, and one part from another, by means of attributes. Hence an object must be thought under the relation of substance and attribute before it is thought under the relation of whole and part. Once more the teacher reaches practical guidance in knowing that the individual must be conceived under these two relations, and in the order named.

THINKING THE INDIVIDUAL THROUGH ATTRIBUTES.

Let us not forget the primary problem in method, as stated at the outset of the discussion on method. It is this : How the mind identifies itself with the object — finds itself in the object; or, what amounts to the same thing, how does it find the object. It does so just in so far as it recognizes its own categories, its own activities, in the object. All the attributes of objects are translatable into mental experiences. They are forms of mental activities as well as defining and limiting marks of the object. It has already been observed that taste in the object thought is also taste in the thinker; and that purpose in the object considered is a mental relation on the part of the one who considers it. The attributes now to be treated are relations between the subject and the object; although naturally, and, therefore, conveniently, we think of them as if they were wholly objective. An attribute may as properly be defined from one side as from the other; thus, an attribute is that which limits and defines the nature of the object; or, viewed from the side of mind, it is that in the mind by which an object is known, or by which one object is distinguished from another. If there were no differences among objects, as shown by their attributes, they could not exist; neither would it be possible to think them.

The foregoing must not suggest that there is no difference between the thinker and the object; this difference cannot be canceled without fusing the subject and the object, and then both vanish. But unless, with this difference, there is a unity of some kind, it is impossible to conceive how the mind could think the object. This may be a mysterious unity; but no less so than the difference. The mind can think only on condition of both. This may be the origin of the mind's law of thinking all things under the relation of diversity and unity. It finally comes to the unity of a self-conscious spirit back of all things; and thus finds for itself the ultimate unity sought, and in which it participates. "Thus, all thinking is a process in which the self finds the self again — the living energy contemplates the living energy under the object." All this is to emphasize the fact that the following attributes, while considered from the objective standpoint, are relations between the thinker and the object.

The primary subdivision of attributes has already been forecast by the thought that every object must be considered in itself and in its relation to other objects; thus giving attributes of (1) Relations, and (2) Properties. These express the two phases of activity in thinking the object, or the two modes of the object's existence. While all attributes are relations, in one class we are conscious of the fact, while in the other we are not. When we think that the sun melts the snow we are conscious of the relation of the sun to the snow; but when we say that the sun is bright, we are not conscious of a relation, but of brightness. The distinction here is one of consciousness and not in fact.

Attributes of Relation. — These are attributes which cannot be thought without bringing into mind some object other than their subject. In thinking of the book on the table, the attribute of position requires the table. Here the book is the subject of the attribute of place. But this attribute of place cannot be conceived in connection with its subject alone. These attributes always distinguish their subject by reference to some other object — by some external limitation; while Properties distinguish their subject by some inherent mark — by some internal limitation. The most fundamental Relation of an object is that of

Purpose and Means. — The purpose, or end, which the object is to serve calls the object into being and unifies its other attributes and parts. These are what they are because of its purpose. The end exists as idea before the object exists as means; but the object exists as means before the end can exist as objective reality. Hence, the end, or purpose, is properly called both first cause and final cause. It is the end which is the beginning, and the beginning which is the end. It is just as proper to say that health promotes exercise as to say that exercise promotes health. Health, held in mind, as idea to be realized, causes one to take exercise, and the exercise causes the real health. Exercise stands between health and health, as caused and causing. The thing created by the idea set up to be realized is a means to the realization of the idea. Thus the object to be considered is created by some idea which the object in turn is to bring forth into the objective world of reality. To study an object under this relation, therefore, is to penetrate to its creative energy; an energy which the mind recognizes as its own. Hence it is through this relation that the mind and the object come into closest unity, as already proposed by the problem of method.

Growing out of the relation of this creative energy to its object are the three attributes, *true, beautiful,* and *good,* depending on whether the intellect, the sensibility, or the will interprets the relation.

There is an idea, a type, an energy which creates the oak. If the intellect perceives the relation of unity between the idea and the reality; if it concludes that the real oak is true to the idea oak, it pronounces the tree true. When we say that he is a true man, it is a true line, or that is a true action, we mean that the real man, line, or action correspond exactly to the idea man, line, or action. The attribute true is the relation of unity, as perceived by the intellect, between the ideal and the real.

If we feel that the idea, in the case of the oak, is not

constrained by the real; if we feel that there is no conflict between what is and what ought to be, we pronounce the tree beautiful. In the acorn, the idea oak is in conflict with the real, with the acorn. The possible oak is in the acorn, and must destroy the acorn to realize itself. But when the perfect tree appears, the ideal and real are one. Then the oak is both ideal and real.

The form of the real must be such as to seem to give freedom to the idea or type within the object. There must be no antagonism, no conflict; the form does not clash with the ideal; the manifestation and the idea are one. The tree, gnarled, twisted, and lopped, seems to do violence to its own nature — to the ideal tree. The perfect form of the tree is felt to be such only because it intuitively suggests the perfection of the idea — that the idea has perfectly realized itself. The germ of every plant bears the imprint of its highest possibilities. The possible plant strives to become actual; when this is felt to be accomplished in the individual tree, it is said to be beautiful, because there is no longer any tension between the ideal and the individual. An infant bears the imprint of its destiny. The idea, or ideal, of manhood strives in it to actualize itself; and when the man's outer life proclaims this to be accomplished — that the possibilities of manhood have become actual in the living person — we are touched with admiration for the beautiful in character. The soul instinctively strives for perfection, and rejoices in its attainment; and by sympathy rejoices in the free manifestation of every ideal. The ultimate ground of the beautiful is the freedom of spirit. The essence of mind, or spirit, is freedom; and by sympathy, through kinship with all nature, the imagination penetrates to the idea, the soul of the object; and the mind rejoices in a like freedom with its own, which it strives to realize. Thus an object is pronounced beautiful through the feeling of sympathy, of freedom, in which the soul finds itself in unity with the object, — the end sought by the process called method in teaching.

A good object is one that accomplishes the end giving rise to the object. In speaking of a good spade, as in speaking of a true or beautiful one, a relation of the spade to its creative idea is expressed; but in "good" there is special reference to fitness of the spade to accomplish the work for which it was designed, and which caused the spade to exist. To view an object as good is to view it in the process of accomplishing its end. The end, as idea, creates the object; the object, in turn, is to realize the idea and is good if adapted to do so. This becomes the ethical quality in persons; the person striving to realize his life purpose. A good man is one who is fulfilling the purpose of his being.

These three attributes, as already stated, do not differ in themselves. The true, the beautiful, and the good are one — the same relation of the ideal to its embodiment. This relation interpreted by the intellect, gives the true; by the sensibility, the beautiful; by the will, the good. The tree is true when the intellect discerns that the real tree corresponds to the ideal; this same tree is beautiful when the emotions respond by sympathy to the freedom of the ideal in the real, based on the fact that the intellect discerns it to be true ; and it is good when our self-activity, as will, interprets the process of it successfully becoming its ideal.

> " . . . Beauty, Good, and Knowledge are three sisters
> That dote upon each other, friends to man,
> Living together under the same roof,
> And never can be sundered without tears."

In these three attributes, the mind meets the object in closest touch. Its own striving to reach its ideal is found in the object. It knows its ideal; is touched by its beauty, and strives to attain it. Every object, as the mind thinks it, has its ideal and its real; the mind, by means of the idealizing power, penetrates it at this point, and finds in it answering elements to its own activity, and pronounces the object true, beautiful, or good.

Cause and Effect.—An object exists in purpose, in thought, before it exists in fact. After a conception of its purpose, a cause must operate to produce the object; and when produced, it acts and reacts on other objects, manifesting itself in effects. Every object is, at the same time, cause and effect. Every event in history is the effect of causes, and is the cause of further effects. The Gulf Stream is at the same time the effect of a cause, and the cause of effects. Cause and effect are dynamical relations ; yet they inhere in the statical object; and are essential to its description. In giving a full conception of the Andes Mountains, as they are at this moment, it may be necessary to think of the forces that upheaved them, and of their effects on climate, vegetable and animal life, and on the industries of man. The relations of cause and effect are the chief relations under which to think a mental state. To bring a mental state fully into consciousness, it is necessary to think of the conditions and circumstances which produce the state; and also to think of the conduct of the person under the influence of the state. To describe a state of fear is to sketch some object that produced that state; as, a tornado whirling aloft the ruined houses of a city, with its effects in the wild gesticulations and screams of the fleeing inhabitants. Spiritual attributes produce an effect on the physical appearance; and the latter, as effect, may be an approach to the former as cause. Physical objects produce an effect on the mind, and are conceived under the relation of effect to the observer. To speak of an object as awful, terrible, stupendous, sublime, picturesque, grotesque, or beautiful, is to think of the object as a cause producing an effect. Irving talks of sober and melancholy days; mournful magnificence; gloomy remains; a picture of glory; amazing height; noiseless reverence; disastrous story; awful harmony; thrilling thunders; solemn concords; and in doing so thinks in terms of effects produced.

Time and Place. — An object cannot be conceived without location in time and place; and it cannot be thus located without reference to another object; hence these are attributes of relation. These answer the questions of the when and the where of the object considered.

Properties.—Properties are attributes which inhere in the nature of the object. They determine it from within, while relations determine it from without. Some properties are essential to the existence of the object as an object, and are involved in every conception of it. Some properties are not necessary to the existence, nor to the conception, of the object. A body may exist and be conceived without taste, smell, odor, sound, or color; but not without extension or the power of resistance. This gives rise to Primary and Secondary properties.

Primary Properties.—These are of two kinds, Extension, the mathematical quality; and Resistance, the physical quality.

Extension gives rise to the Form and Size of objects; the first resulting from the kind, the second from the degree, of extension. These relations unify the other attributes to the senses, as purpose does to thought. The weight, color, taste, odor, coincide within the same form and limit. Extension is the empty form of the object, which the other attributes are to fill out. The object in its relation of position, form, and size being wholly passive, these relations are properly called *statical*. These, after purpose, are most commonly used to distinguish objects. They distinguish physical objects in a literal sense; but spiritual objects in a figurative sense. We speak of a large-minded man; of a man "four square to all the winds that blow"; of a straight man; of a right- and wrong-headed man; of men superior and inferior; of high-minded men.

Resistance adds to the idea of a mere extended form that of a power which resists the muscular sense. A resisting as well as an extending something, is essential to our notion of being. If the reality of an object is doubted, the question is settled by testing its power of resistance. If there is no resistance we pronounce the object an illusion, however positively the other senses may affirm their verdict. A ghost deceives all the senses but one.

This general attribute of resistance manifests itself in particular objects, as hard, soft, fluid, firm, tough, brittle, rigid, flexible, rough, smooth, light, heavy, compressible, incompressible, elastic, non-elastic, etc. — the physical properties of matter, as the others were the mathematical. It is obvious that these attributes are given by the muscular sense; the lowest sense giving the most fundamental quality. This sense, through these primary qualities of resistance, brings us into a knowledge of external existence. While the spatial relations condition the existence of matter as such, these are the inner forces which determine and distinguish all objects as objects. They are not determined from without, but are themselves the shaping and conditioning forces. These forces reveal themselves only in reaction against a force within ourselves ; and with them we begin our struggle with the outer world. These physical attributes, which are manifested in the struggle with the material world, are the ones attributed to spirit in its struggle in the moral world; such as firm, rigid, resisting, flexible, stern, unyielding, stable, resolute, strong, lenient, persistent, austere, rigorous, etc.

Attributes of resistance include not only passive resistance but active resistance — resistance rising into self-activity and will. The will is the analogue of muscular resistance. Man, in putting aside allurements or in facing dangers in order to hold to his ideal worth, displays the attribute of resistance in a much higher degree than the stone in his pathway, which, because hard and heavy, he shuns. Resistance, properly considered, is the highest manly virtue. A man must stand for something and against something. The degree of force with which this is done marks his manhood. This relation of resistance, after rising into self-activity, is the one employed in thinking all mental phenomena. The mind can be known only as a self-active power. In describing a man's faculties of intellect, or his sensibility or will, it must be done in terms of free activity. Thus there is the same relation for thinking a material and a spiritual object. This power of resistance rises gradually into the form of self-activity. The plant has more of this than the clod from which it springs; the animal has more than the plant; and the man more than either. The mind can limit itself and thus become the object of its own activity. Being able to think itself, it manifests a higher form of activity than any other object.

The subject and the object both being active, these attributes are called *statico-dynamical.*

Secondary Properties.— These are less essential to the object. They are felt to be affections of the senses rather than qualities of the object. Sound is felt to be subjective; while firmness, given by the muscular sense, is felt to be in the object. The muscular sense gives an objective resisting something, which as cause produces a subjective effect on the sense of touch, taste, smell, hearing, and sight; giving rise to the various tactile sensations, tastes, odors, sounds, and colors. These senses cannot reveal to us the objective world; unless the sense of sight be an exception, coöperating with the muscular sense to give externality and form. With this exception, these secondary attributes produce their effect on the senses through an active condition of the body to which the attributes belong. The object, to be tasted or smelt, must be in a state of dissolution; and to be heard, in a state of motion. Sight and touch are more nearly like the muscular sense in that they present the body in its normal condition; yet light is conveyed to the eye through the vibration of the particles of the body, and the same is true of some forms of tactile sensations.

These attributes grade upward in this order: touch, taste, smell, hearing, and sight. In this ascending order, the object becomes more and more active and the observer more and more passive. Also, the closeness of contact of the observer with the object diminishes in passing from touch to sight; or, as the distance of the object from the observer increases. In touch, the contact is close; in sight it may be as remote as the stars. Again, the definiteness of location and specialization of function increases from touch to sight; the sense of touch being distributed over the body, while the sense of sight is focused at a point.

The organ of touch has other functions than that of touch; but the eye is relieved from all duties but that of sight. But more to the present purpose, this ascending order of attributes is ascending in importance in thinking the object. Sight and sound reveal more fully the nature of an object than do odor and taste. In sight the object is active, making this attribute near to that of active resistance. The same is true of sound, but in a less degree. There is more resistance and activity in a flash of lightning than in a clap of thunder.

Since the object is active, affecting the subject, these attributes are properly called *dynamical*.

The attributes are secondary only in the sense that they are less essential to the existence of the object. If the basis were the effect on the mind, the order would be reversed; for sight and hearing stand first in that they minister to the wants of the soul; while taste and smell minister to the wants of the body; and the other attributes, to the necessities of the object.

Thus the muscular sense stands at one extreme of the sense scale, giving that which is of first importance to the object; and hearing and sight at the other, giving that which is of first importance to the mind.

The terms used to name physical qualities are freely used metaphorically to name spiritual qualities. In fact, all words descriptive of spiritual objects originally signified physical attributes. Those that seem now to be applied literally, as calm, candid, pure, sincere, bright, dull, etc., have simply lost their physical analogy through constant use.

Viewing now the whole list of attributes, it may be observed that it constitutes an ascending order from mere tactile sensation and taste to purpose. And this is not only an ascending order of attributes, but, as might be expected from the unity between the mind and its object, it is an ascending order of activities by which these attributes are grasped. Touching or tasting is a lower order of activity than that required in grasping coöperation of means to end. Besides, the lower, sensuous activities cannot grasp the larger complex individuals. Sight cannot make one aware of a state, as it can of a house; and taste can reveal to the mind an orange, but not the organized orange industry. The senses which give the secondary attributes cannot enter the higher realm. Mind alone reigns there.

From tactile sensation and taste to resistance and extension, inclusive, the knowledge comes by observation — through sense-impressions made by the outer world. This is the field of observation lessons, and introduces the lower phase of work with natural objects — object lessons. It is well to insist here on the systematic training to thorough, accurate, and methodical observation; for such activity and habit are necessary to bring the mind into the unity of truth with the object. Thorough observation (thorough = through) means that the pupil uses the complete circle of the senses on the complete circle of properties; accurate observation means that each attribute be discriminated from the other attributes and from the same attributes in other objects; and methodical observation means that each attribute must be taken in the order in which it is needed by the mind in constituting the object. The mind naturally begins observing with muscular sense, including touch, and through these arrives at form and size. Then, into the resisting something having form, it puts, fuses, the other attributes, beginning with the attribute given by the eye. Thus the object is given individuality, in which the other attributes inhere. The following from Hickok's Mental Science exemplifies the method of observation: "Then this (a large crystal of salt) is taken under the pressure of muscular touch, the property of a hard impenetrability is at once perceived, and when the pressure has been spread over the entire surface, the cubic form of the crystal will be given in connection with the hardness. If the light falling on the cubic crystal be reflected to the eye in a scientific experiment, there will be the perception of a gray color taking the cubic form and connecting itself with the hard crystal of the touch in exact coincidence. If the hard, colored crystal be stricken together with another and aerial reverberations reach the ear, there will be perceived the noisy click of the percussion put directly as a property of sound within the colored cubic hardness. If this, again, be carried to the tongue, there will further be perceived an acrid taste, and when all is yet further brought to the nose, there will, with the taste, also be a saline odor, and both the acrid taste and the bitter smell will be consciously connected with the formerly perceived properties. The crystal will now be recognized as hard, and cubic, and gray, and acrid, and with a saline smell, and a clicking sound. It has now gone the circuit of the attending senses and the property of each having been joined, each respectively to the other, all are now concentratively connected in the one crystal."

Thus let the student be required to observe thoroughly and in order, such objects as a piece of cork, rubber, stone, chalk, metal, a leaf, an apple, etc. In this exercise the logical order of attributes must be strictly adhered to. If the purpose of the object is given, the order of the attributes will be determined by the order of their relation to that purpose. If this is not given, as in the example above, the order will be determined by the physical constitution of the object. This is the best of language drills, especially by way of forcing to a full and accurate vocabulary. The student is thus put on the stress for attributive words to express the various forms, sizes, kinds, resistances, colors, sounds, tastes, and odors of objects. Such physical observation leads naturally into the chemical and physical laboratory, where ordinary observation is aided by experiments.

The attributes through which the object is grasped by sense-observation, make it picturable to the imagination. The imagination is more fruitful in presenting objects than is the faculty of observation. The picturing faculty is made accurate, full, and strong on a basis of thorough training in sense-observation, as well as by systematic training in its own kind of observation. This kind of observation should receive as careful training as the other. Opportunities are offered in all lines of work. This is prominently true in geography and history.

The sensuous object ceases in the attribute of resistance. Out of the material furnished by the senses the mind constructs the object in space and time — its position, form, and size. Cause and effect are not perceivable or picturable. These relations must be grasped by the understanding. Purpose and means, in the form of the true, beautiful, and the good, are apprehended by the intuition of reason. Thus the scheme of attributes appears in an ascending order from taste to purpose. And this suggests the important thought that this order of attributes is an ascending scale of thinking the universal into the individual. Tasting an object puts little meaning into it; hearing gives more of its internal and essential constitution; its relation to other objects as manifested in cause and effect is still more significant; and when its purpose is reached, its mental intention, its fullest nature is disclosed. This ascending order means closer and closer unity of the thinker with the object. When an object is said to be bitter or pungent, or hard or square, it seems quite other than the self; but when adaptation to some ideal end is reached, there is at once a feeling of kinship with the object. This is shown by the increasing delight accompanying the upward ascent of thought. When the pupils feel that there is adjustment to some design, he has met most intimately his own life in the object.

The preceding suggests a great truth of method in education. The pupil's spiritual life must be aided to transcend his sensuous life; and more, his sensual life. This can be done by revealing to him the pure mental delight in the higher relations of objects. The mathematical relations, those of cause and effect, and purpose and means, in the true, beautiful, and good, are free from all sensuality.

Finally, a significant fact, and one full of guidance in teaching, must be noted. When an object is viewed under all the properties and relations noted, it is not necessarily exhaustively considered. The properties and relations— especially the relations—may be completely listed, but the fact that each has wider and still wider degree of generality, has not been stated. Purpose, and cause and effect are of two kinds, immediate and remote, with all degrees of remoteness. The immediate cause and effect of the Declaration of Independence are quite different from its remote cause and effect; and they are as much less significant as they are less remote. The more remotely we take its bearings, either in its origin or its end, the more deeply do we penetrate it. The cotton-gin is to gin cotton; so much is easy, and so much the child can think; but its ultimate purpose in the spiritual development of man is a problem for the philosopher. The cause of the Mississippi River, in the immediate rainfall of its valley, is matter for the primary geography class; but its remote cause in geologic and meteorological forces of the world engages the full power of the university student. The form of this particular cone is an elementary truth, and easy to comprehend until that form is to be reduced to its ultimate mathematical law. That an object is hard or soft, light or heavy, is found immediately in the object and by direct sense-perception; but self-activity and spiritual resistance are remote, subtle, and complex.

Therefore, let it not be supposed that because an object is considered under all the foregoing properties and relations, that the object is thoroughly or exhaustively considered. Thorough thinking requires the mind to view an object under all its relations, or through all that the purpose of the thinking requires; but this should include the pushing of each relation to the limit of the power exercised in grasping that relation. Any pupil, even in the first grade, may think an object under all the properties and relations noted; but no university student will be able to push those same properties and relations to their ultimate limit. Each pupil must push the relations out as far as his ability will permit. The teacher must exhaust the pupil, but not the object. Exhaustive teaching may apply to the student, but never to the subject. The teacher beholds a wealth of relations beyond the reach of the student; and the student may get a glimpse of the promised land, which increased knowledge and discipline alone will enable him to enter.

THINKING THE INDIVIDUAL BY MEANS OF PARTS.

The grasping of an object as a whole under the relation of substance and attribute is followed by its analysis into parts. This process is called *partition*. Thus there are two phases of the process of thinking the individual: the *attributive* phase and the *partitive* phase.

The object to be described is a unity of complex ideas — attributes and parts. Growing out of this fact, the law of thinking is, that the mind must grasp the object in its unity of these ideas. The law of unity which controls in attributive description is now to control partitive description. The object being a unit composed of organic parts, the mind must analyze it into parts, and then synthesize the parts into their organic unity. This law of organic unity through analysis and synthesis requires the student—

1. *To think the object into parts on the same basis of division;*

2. *To think the parts in the order determined by the basis;*

3. *To think all the parts which the basis determines.*

1. Every object has some unifying idea. This may be the relation of parts in space, the order in which they occur to the eye, or some fundamental principle. The first two are the mere outer form of unity; the operation of the fundamental principle produces the real unity.

In dividing an individual there is a choice of bases, determined by the purpose of the description. It may serve the purpose best to follow some accidental basis, as the order in which the parts appear to the eye, or the relative position in space. Such obvious and superficial bases are always used in the lower order of descriptions — descriptions in which the sensuous phase of the object is made prominent. The more scientific the description, the more fundamental the basis. This is a question of adaptation to a purpose. On the basis of separation in space, the child readily divides the human body into head, trunk, and limbs. And this is the best basis for the child, but the physiologist would insist on a basis more intimately connected with life processes. The ordinary description of a landscape would require the mention of such parts as appear at different places, or as occur at different moments of time. But for geopraphical purposes, the basis must be some fundamental relation to life. Every change in the basis gives a new set of parts.

Not only does this law require the basis to be chosen which is best adapted to the purpose of the teaching, but it requires that all the parts be determined on the same basis.

If a teacher should present a tree as composed of root, bark, trunk, woody substance, branches, and pith ; or the human body as composed of flesh, blood, nerves, muscular tissue, vital organs, adipose tissue, bone, and mechanical system, using two or more bases of division, utter confusion would arise in the mind of the learner. The divisions should be such as could be made of the actual object. The tree can be actually parted into root, trunk, and branches, putting each part in a different place. So with pulpy matter, woody substance, and pith. But if one should attempt to make an actual division of the tree on both bases at once, he would have a practical illustration of what the law of unity means in requiring the divisions to be made on the same basis.

2. Having determined the parts by the same basis, the parts must be presented in the order in which they are

found in the object, as determined by the adopted basis. To present the parts of a tree as roots, leaves, trunk, and branches, would cause the mind to form an object wholly different from the one to be described.

The basis of partition used determines the order of presenting the parts. It is not necessarily an order of nearness in space, or succession in time. It may be an order of functional relation. When the basis of division is that of space, the parts must be named in spatial order. When the basis of division is the order of observation in time, the parts must be named in the order of occurrence. When the basis is some determining principle, the parts must be named in their functional relation, without regard to their position or succession. Thus the parts of the eyeball may be named from without inward, or from within outward, following an order in space; or, following the operation of the law of optics, there would be an entirely different method of procedure; as, first, the retina; second, the crystalline lens, with the parts about it which aid in refracting light; then those parts which regulate the light; followed by those which adjust and protect the image-forming parts.

3. Not only must the parts be determined by the same basis and presented methodically, but all the parts determined by the basis must be enumerated. To present a tree as composed of trunk, branches, and leaves; or a flower as composed of calyx, corolla, and pistil, is to present the mind with an incomplete unit; and hence, a violation of the general law of unity.

Thus the basis being determined by the purpose, if all such parts as the basis gives be presented in the order of their relation as determined by the basis, the mind will the more readily and correctly organize them into the unity they were before their necessary separation in the process of presentation.

Strict adherence to the foregoing laws of partition will train the pupil to the power of grasping an object clearly; *i.e.*, the power of thinking the individual into parts, and, at the same time of thinking the parts into their organic unity. The teacher will not need to seek an opportunity for this kind of drill; for it will of necessity occur daily. In treating such objects as an eye, a thermometer, a ship, an engine, a bird, a human body, a landscape, a legislature, etc., he must apply the process of partition; and the more rigidly this is done the greater the power of analysis conferred and the more accurate the knowledge gained. The power of analysis does not at all mean the power of mere separation: it means the power of seeing parts as parts of a whole. Power of analysis means coördinating and organizing power.

After the analysis of an object into parts, the attributes of each part must be given according to the law of presenting attributes as a whole. Such attributes of each part must be given as will show its organic relation in the object as a whole. If the basis of separation is that of purpose, the separation into parts would be followed by such attributes of each part as fit it to its function. A different basis would not only give different parts, but different attributes of those parts would be required. When the basis of partition is the appearance of the parts to the eye, the picture-making attributes of color and form of each part must be emphasized.

THINKING ONE INDIVIDUAL BY MEANS OF ANOTHER.

In thinking the attributes and parts of an object, the relation of the object's likeness and difference is prominently and effectively employed. The mental processes involved are those of *comparison* and *contrast*.

In its most abbreviated form, comparison is made by throwing the object into its class. The first question which arises concerning an object is, What is it? That is, What is it like? The answer is given by naming the class to which the object belongs. Often a detailed process of thought may be avoided by stating that the object under discussion is like some well-known object, or belongs to a well-known class. This economizes the thought processes by substituting the results of former processes. Without requiring the mind to think anew the action of the valves in a vein, the attention may be called to the valve of a pump, this being known.

A strange fruit may be put before the mind at once by comparing it to an apple, if essentially like it, and thus save wearisome details in both language and thought. To refer a strange animal to its species saves a volume of descriptive detail and a useless repetition of thought processes. The implied comparison presents the essential character of the object, and if the special marks of the individual are required, a few points of contrast will fill the outline. Of two objects equally well known, comparison and contrast is a strong means of presenting and deepening a knowledge of each. Often a vivid and sufficient description may be made by presenting the object in contrast with its extreme opposite. Besides, comparing an object with its opposite forces the mind to essential truth in the object studied.

1. The purpose in comparison and contrast requires that the proper object, and the proper attributes and parts of the object, be chosen with which to compare the theme. The purpose being to abbreviate thought processes, the object chosen must be (1) a familiar object, and (2) must have the greatest number of points common to the theme.

To select an object less familiar than the theme, or points of comparison that need explanation themselves, is to defeat the purpose of the comparison. In order that the object may have the greatest number of points common to the theme it must not be chosen from a class more comprehensive than necessary. The comparison of a horse with a reptile would violate this law. Both belong to vertebrates; but it would be better to choose from mammals, as the bat; better still to choose from quadrupeds, as the lion; and still better to choose from the ungulata, as the ox.

2. A second law requires that the points of likeness and difference be presented in the order of their relation, as required by the law of unity in presenting attributes and parts. A point of likeness may be given, and then

a corresponding point of difference; thus carrying the likenesses and differences in parallel lines. Or, all the likenesses may be given by themselves, and the differences by themselves.

3. The law of completeness requires that all points of likeness and difference be given which are necessary to present the theme fully.

Skill in comparison and contrast can be secured by such practice as will require the conscious application of the laws here named.

There is no more effective means of assigning work than that of requiring the pupil to compare and contrast the object under consideration with a given object or objects. No special opportunity for this need be sought; it occurs in almost every lesson. In studying Africa the pupil can do no better than to compare it with South America; or Jupiter with the Earth; Washington with Lincoln; the English government with that of the United States.

Thinking the Individual as Changing.

This gives the time whole as distinguished from the space whole. A time whole consists of all the attributes and parts which the object has manifested in a period of time. Wherever there is change there must be permanence. Something that endures through all changes can be conceived only as such in connection with the changing. The brook flows on; changes perpetually:—

> "Men may come and men may go,
> But I go on forever."

The same brook goes on forever. A man grows from infancy to old age; many changes take place, but there is the abiding ego, the subject of all change. He does not lose his identity. The earth has moved from a molten mass to its present organized form; attributes and parts have come and gone; but the same earth remained through all. In all the changes of human history there has been a continuity of human life. Thus, change means permanence; something that abides but manifests itself in varying features through a period of time. This permanent something taken with the sum of its varying manifestations through a period of time constitutes the time whole. In the space whole the object was considered as the sum of its attributes and parts at a given moment, as it were by a cross section; but in the time whole the sum is taken lengthwise the life of the object.

To study a thing as changing forces to the discovery of the permanent, the essential in the object. The changes are not noted for their own sake; the abiding amidst changes may be discerned. This plant or the constitution of the United States cannot be known except in the light of their development. Education is studied in its history to find what is essential in its methods. Nothing brings one so close to the life of a man or a nation as to study the changes from infancy to manhood.

The foregoing discloses not only the value of this process of thinking an object, but also the method of thinking it. Its variations must be held into the unity of the unchanging something. As in the description of an object the greatest diversity of attributes possible, and of parts, were bound into the unity of the individual as it existed at a given moment, so the greatest diversity of attributes and parts is to be bound into the unity of the individual between two points of time. This is the law of unity in thinking the changing individual.

Thus again, as in description, the mental movement as a whole is that of analysis and synthesis. The different elements existing at different times must be selected and synthesized into the unity of the whole. This unity is established by means of the following threads of relation, all of which are involved in every conception of change.

Purpose. — A conception of change involves the idea of end, or purpose, which the change is to accomplish. Purpose, prompting and guiding every movement, is both the beginning and the end of every change. The need of a reaper is felt; and this prompts to a purpose to satisfy the need through an invention. This purpose institutes a series of changes in the object to meet the need which prompted to the purpose. Hence, it may be said that purpose is the moving force in a series of changes; and that in narration, as in description, it is the most fundamental thought-relation. But purpose in narration differs from purpose in description. In narration it is viewed as bringing the object into reality; while in description it is viewed as the work to be done by the already existing object. Purpose creates the mowing machine, but when created, the machine may be viewed as adapted to the work to be done.

Time.—A conception of change involves the idea of time, as a conception of attributes and parts in the fixed object involves the idea of space. A change cannot take place except in time; and cannot be conceived without its time-relations. Therefore, time, answering the questions when and how long, is one of the fundamental thought-relations in narrating an object. Time is necessary to explain not only the relation of each event in a series to every other; but also to explain the entire change with reference to other events. An event in history may be accounted for by its relation in time to preceding or succeeding events. In fact, it cannot be explained without this relation. The relation of preceding, succeeding, and during, one or all, are absolutely essential to the explanation of an event. Time has already been noted as one of the relations essential in thinking a fixed object; but it is more prominently, and differently, employed in viewing a changing object. In this, periods are marked; succession is given.

Cause and Effect.—The changes in objects are produced by causes; and the changes themselves produce effects. Every conception of a change involves the idea of cause and effect. To think the manufacture of a lead pencil, the growth of a tree, the development of character, or the progress of civil liberty, requires, as an element in the conception, the forces operative in each case to produce the changes, with the result produced. Therefore, cause and effect must be added to the fundamental thought-relations in grasping a changing object. Cause and effect, employed in thinking a fixed object, are differently employed in thinking the changing object. In this they are viewed as determining changes; but in the other they were used to show the fixed nature of the object. When it is said that paint improves houses the effect is given to show the nature of paint, and not for the change produced.

Whole and Part.—The relation of whole and part, as in the coexistent object, is the most prominent thought-relation in a successive object. The parts are the changes themselves; and these must be kept prominently before the mind in the application of all other relations. Besides, in most objects the changes thrust themselves on the attention. They may be seen and heard; while the other relations reveal themselves only to thought. It is easy to picture the panorama of events in a battle; but causes, results, and purposes can be ascertained only by reflection.

It is more difficult to obey the laws of partition in the changing object than in the fixed object, for the parts in this case are successive, or time parts. Time is a continuous quantity, while a space object is discrete. Hence, the divisions of time are more or less arbitrary; while in most space objects, nature marks the divisions. The shifting of a dividing line in time one hundred years will often do no violence to the purpose of the narration. Because there are no distinct separations in time, which the mind requires for convenience in thinking, an artificial system is adopted; and the divisions of time by the calendar, satisfying in the sharpness of its boundaries, stand ready made to cut events into parts of definite and convenient length. But whether this arbitrary exactness or some inner moving principle be adopted as the basis will be determined by the purpose of the narration. That basis must be chosen which will best accomplish the purpose of the narration. If the history of England be narrated to show the course of civil freedom, the law of selection would be violated in choosing the reign of kings as a basis of separation. This would be a proper basis, if, instead of their inner life, the external phase of things is desired. For common purposes of narration, the external separation of events by some accidental accompaniment, as the above, is proper; but for the highest purpose, the phases that mark the progress of the moving principle in the realization of itself must be chosen as the basis. In such a movement there are no definite boundaries; and to make the arbitrary distinctions of date or king control the presentation is to do violence to the purpose. The picturesque phase of things may well mark the divisions of a child's history; but in tracing for the mature, the movement towards spiritual freedom, the basis of the division must be the relation of that movement to the end.

The law of method requires the parts to be presented in the order of occurrence. Whatever the basis of division, this order, except for the special reason of giving results preparatory to their explanation, cannot be violated. When the arbitrary divisions of time are made, the events must follow in the order of time; if cause and effect be made the basis, effect must follow cause; and if purpose, the end is realized by a series of movements in time.

The law of completeness requires that all the changes be presented which are necessary, under the conditions, to the purpose of the narration.

Likeness and Difference.—Every change involves a comparison and contrast of the object with itself at a preceding or a succeeding moment. Therefore, likeness and difference belong to the list of fundamental thought-relations in narrating an object. This relation is not only essential to the conception of a change, but it is used, as in description, to facilitate the thought processes under all other relations. Well known events may be used in comparison to explain an event under discussion. This not only shortens the narrative process, but it deepens the impression. For this reason, two events equally well known may be compared and contrasted with great advantage.

Changes may be compared under all of the thought-relations above—purpose, time, cause, effect, and parts. Objects differ in the relations named; and this process is a means of presenting each of the relations. Which relation shall be selected to be thus presented is determined by the purpose of the narration as a whole.

We have now discussed in outline the universal process of thinking the individual.

THOUGHT-RELATIONS CONSTITUTING THE INDIVIDUAL.

I. As coexistent, or fixed.
    1. By means of Attributes.
        a. Relations.
            (1) Purpose and Means. { True. Beautiful. Good. }
            (2) Cause and Effect.
            (3) Time and Place.
        b. Properties.
            (1) Primary.
                a. Extension. { Form. Size. }
                b. Resistance. { Active. Passive. }
            (2) Secondary.
                a. Color.
                b. Sound.
                c. Odor.
                d. Taste.
                e. Mere Tactile Sensation.
    2. As made up of Parts.
        a. Analysis by the laws of Partition.
        b. Attributes of each part as of the whole.

II. As successive, or changing.
    1. As a whole, under the relation of
        a. Purpose.
        b. Time. (Place may be required.)
        c. Cause and Effect.
        d. Likeness and Difference.
    2. As composed of Parts.
        a. Analysis into parts by the laws of Partition.
        b. Each part presented under the relations of the whole.

APPLICATION OF THE FOREGOING EXPOSITION.

The foregoing is a universal outline of the mind's movement, or method, of thinking an individual. This complete circle of relations in the object answers the complete circle of activities in the learner. One phase of the object is grasped by sense perception; one, by the understanding; one, by reason. The mere individuality of the object as limited in space or time is made known through the senses, or picturing imagination; the organic unit, or thought whole, of the object is known through the understanding; while reason, as intuition, pronounces the object true, beautiful, or good, when measured by some ideal set up by the mind itself.

In practice, the first step is to sketch all the relations constituting the object, and the activities by which the relations are grasped. Such is a kind of universal preparation for teaching the object, and must precede such a plan of lesson as is given under the "illustration of the teaching process" pages 11 to 29. But when the teacher is to instruct a given class of pupils, a modifying factor arises; and this requires a revision of the previous universal outline. The pupils' knowledge and discipline are not sufficient to enable them to think the object under all of its relations. This same fact may prevent teaching the relations in their logical order; or from seizing the object in its organic unity. So that the laws of unity, method, selection, and completeness must be applied in the light of the condition of the children's minds at the time of the instruction. Thus the object to be taught has an order of relations independent of the thinking of any particular mind; and this order is the universal factor of all lessons to be given on the object. This given class, with its known development, is the particular factor determining a given lesson.

APPLICATION I. — AMAZON RIVER.

First Step. — Resolving the river into its constituent thought-relations — the universal factor.

I. *The Amazon River as fixed.* — 1. The End the river serves; (a) immediate, such as drainage of a designated part of South America, and as a highway of travel; (b) remote, as advancement of civilization, even remote good in the development of the race. Perhaps its highest use is that to the mind itself, as a clean cut type of the unity of physical forces, and as an emblem of life. In this latter view, the use of the river is that of mere expression. This brings it into the field of the beautiful, by making the individual stand for a universal. Here the mind comes into closest unity with the river.

2. Cause and Effect must be noted under the two heads of immediate and remote. Its immediate cause is in the rainfall of South America; which rainfall is conditioned by the contour and trade winds of South America. Hence, contour and trade winds are remote causes, one degree removed from the immediate cause. Passing out from these, still more remote causes are found in the surroundings of South America; and then in the form and

revolution of the earth. The sun, moon, and stars are causative agents in the Amazon River. The effect, immediate and remote, must likewise be traced.

3. Time here means nothing more than the Amazon River as now viewed; and not the river as it was centuries ago. But this is implied and needs no remark in the outline. Under Place should be given its absolute location, by latitude and longitude; and relative as to South America, including its direction.

4. Under Extension, as to form, the course of the river must be traced from its mouth to its source; as to size, its length, breadth, and depth must be noted — breadth and depth at different points, including stream and channel, at both the wet and the dry season.

5. Under Resistance, the current at different points and the mighty force of its volume of water are to be noted; especially in its effect on the Atlantic Ocean.

6. Of the secondary attributes, color is the only one essential in thinking the river.

7. Treating this object by Partition is simple. A river is water flowing in a channel. A conception of a river includes both the stream and the channel. Hence, the parts are stream and channel, the basis being that of resistance; the one confining the other — the relation of confined and confining.

The next step must note the attributes and the parts of the parts. It will be observed that this has already been included in the description of the river as a whole, except the parts of the channel. These include the bed and the banks; which should be given as under the attributes of the whole. The banks must be extended back to include the magnificent forests, and the sweep of the river at high water.

II. *The Amazon as changing.* — 1. So far as can now be discovered the river as it now is was the End toward which the geologic forces creating the Amazon tended.

2. Under Time must be given the period from its beginning to the present. Under Place, note shifting positions during its time.

3. Under Cause and Effect, the geologic forces which made it a river, and brought it to its present condition.

4. Likenesses and Differences to formation of other rivers.

5. Under Parts must be noted the stages of the river's evolution, and through what stages it will yet pass.

Second Step. — Modifications of foregoing outline by limitations, in knowledge and discipline, of class to be taught — the particular factor.

The mental processes of seizing each of the foregoing relations must be set over against the relation to be seized. For instance, if the pupil could be present and traverse the country, sense-perception would give the properties, the individualizing marks. If not present, the picturing imagination must create the magnificent image — sublime in its length, breadth, and luxuriance of vegetable and animal life. A low form of judgment through inference is required in forming the foregoing picture, and in discerning the immediate relation of cause and effect. The pupil will picture the rapid flow down the slope of the Andes, and the sluggish flow and widening expanse toward the mouth by means of inference, and should not be aided to do so by testimony of book or teacher. In grasping the more remote causes and results, a more complex and involved form of judgment is required. The judgment necessary to connect the contour of South America with the river is one degree more complex and involved than that required in connecting the rainfall. In one, the relation is seen between the objects; in the other, between the relations between objects. Still more complex is the activity in connecting the form and motions of the earth with the river. Such requires simple judgment raised to the fourth power — grasping relations between relations, which are relations between other relations; and these again are relations between relations between objects. To perceive the river as an expression of the unity of all physical forces and a symbol of life and destiny, requires the intuition of reason. There is a low degree of this, however, that is not beyond a primary pupil.

Coming now to a supposed class to be taught, say a fourth-reader class, let it be noted that they are in the following condition of mind in relation to the subject: —

1. As to knowledge, in general, they know the geographical elements; as, river, mountain, valley, rainfall. In particular, they know the exact and relative location, vertical and horizontal form of South America, and the winds blowing over it.

2. As to faculties developed, the picturing imagination is active, and the judgment is one or two degrees removed from simple judgment. Under these conditions, what modifications need to be made in the universal outline?

First, the river as a successive individual must be omitted, because these pupils have no knowledge upon which to base the thinking required; and the forces are too remote, and too wide in their reach, to be grasped by the order of judgment possessed. The remote causes and results, and purposes and means must also be canceled. The cause cannot be traced further into the universal force than the trade winds and the relief of the continent; and the effect must be limited to that on the physical country immediately surrounding, and on the immediate industries.

The pupil will be strong in forming the picture of the individual Amazon by means of its properties — form, size, resistance in its flow, color; and its parts, including especially its banks, with their dense vegetation and teeming animal life. This picture Amazon imaged under these picture relations, together with a narrow circle of relations connecting it with the world, constitutes the subject-matter for our class. The natural order for this is the formation of the picture first, and then the connection of the river with the forces forming it.

Third Step. — The teacher is now prepared to state the lesson in full, as in the example pages 12 to 30; and which is given below in suggestive and briefest possible outline: —

The mental process as a whole.—From the general notion river, to the notion of this particular river, by means of their knowledge of South America, already suggested.

Steps in the process: —

1. Imaging the position of the Amazon.
2. Imaging the form.
3. Imaging the size, $\begin{cases} \text{length,} \\ \text{breadth,} \\ \text{depth,} \end{cases}$ at different seasons. at different places.
4. Imaging the flow at different points. (Inference involved.)
5. Imaging the color. (Inference involved.)
6. Analysis into parts, and each part treated under such attributes as are not involved in the foregoing, giving much attention to the dense life on the banks.
7. Reasoning out the river as now pictured, inferring its position, form, size, etc., from the extent, relief, and winds of South America.
8. Transforming the river into a type of human life. The teacher should keep in poetic mood; pupils are always poets. With a little help, the pupil will readily suggest truths of life which the river reflects. It is a pulsating thing, rhythmical to the earth's heart-beats of physical forces. It, like the sluggish, muddy Concord, as given by Hawthorne, mirrors ideally the foliage on its banks, and the sky and clouds above — mirrors the heaven that broods over it. "All the sky glows downward at our feet, the rich clouds float through the unruffled bosom of the stream like heavenly thoughts through a peaceful

heart. We will not, then, malign our river as gross and impure while it can glorify itself with so adequate a picture of the heaven that broods above it; or, if we remember its tawny hue and the muddiness of its bed, let it be a symbol that the earthliest human soul has an infinite spiritual capacity and may contain the better world within its depths."

Means in the process. — In general, a good descriptive text, magazine articles, books on the Amazon, and good maps are needed. The pupil may infer much. It is well to note here the difference between assigning a lesson by so much of text, and by points to be worked out, which compel the pupil to use the text, the reference-book, and every other means at his command. This at one stroke stops rote learning by compelling the pupil to think the thing itself.

Educational value of the process. — This value should be stated in light of the universal aim of education, and the universal laws by which the mind grows. The magnificent panorama of picture is an illuminating presence in the soul; making full and rich the conscious life of the child, — a presence crowding out things ugly and unworthy; an inner resource against the dullness and monotony of life; an impulse against the temptations and allurements along life's pathway. To form this picture means more than a mere knowledge of the Amazon; it means inner life and resource to the pupil. It means not only richness of coloring and wealth of picture as if to the eye, but sublime mood to the soul, from contemplating the majestic flow and yearly pulsation through sublime forests and interminable plains. And then, when the picture is transformed into a type of universal life, it is held before the pupil not merely as a picture but as a revelation of his own life. It then has truly life meaning and life potency in it. And further, when the pupil perceives this river as the coöperation of forces external to itself, he has a form of thought by which he is finally to resolve all the forces of the world into the unity of a single force. Nothing brings more elation to the soul than to feel its way towards such unity.

These few statements on the plan of a lesson on the Amazon are meant only to connect the foregoing laws with the individual teaching act as described in the first chapter. The teacher should expand this outline as formally and as fully as the example on the pyramid; and more so, for it may now be done in light of the universal law, so far as discussed. Thus we have returned to the point of starting — from the individual teaching act, through the universal law in two of its phases, to the individual act. There is this difference between the two individual acts; in the last, the teacher may see the process of thinking the Amazon as a universal process; and its educational value as a universal value.

We must not fail to note here, also, the connection of this detailed process of thinking the Amazon with the universal law of method, previously stated. By that law the mind moves from the individual out toward the universal, and back to the individual, discerning at last the universal in the individual. The foregoing illustration exhibits in detail the phases of movement in bringing the individual into unity with the universal. The teacher should not lose sight of the larger movement in the details of the process. In every step, the teacher should be conscious of pressing toward the universal.

The foregoing example illustrates again the principle of gradation in school. The Amazon as a mere picture is a fit topic for primary pupils; in its narrow circle of relations it is suitable for grammar grades; still wider relations for the high-school pupil; and the university student may exhaust his powers on what remains.

APPLICATION II. — A HEART.

For further illustration, and to exhibit more strictly the law of unity in the method of thought, suppose a heart is to be taught. Making out at once the relations and steps suitable to a common-school class, the following appears: —

Steps in the Process. — I. *Thinking the heart as fixed,* and under the unifying idea of purpose and means. Purpose, to circulate the blood through all parts of the body.

1. Perceiving, or imagining, position; judgment aiding. This position should be noted (1) with reference to the body as a whole, and (2) with reference to other organs, especially the lungs, and the veins and arteries. But the essential thing to note here is that the pupil must unify the position as above given with the primary attri-

bute of the heart, purpose. He must think the position as a means to the purpose. This requires no high order of judgment, and may be done by a primary class.

2. Perceiving form, aided by comparison with similar forms. Next, the form must be thought as means to the end of circulation. The fact of its being hollow easily connects with its use ; and if the form were anything else, in general, but spherical, it could not have power to force the blood.

3. Perceiving size, exactly, and relatively to body and force required to propel the blood ; thus relating size as means to the heart's use.

4. Inferring its resistance — its contractile power — from its size and the force required. Its rhythmical and automatic action described. This attribute of contractility should be noted as the attribute most immediate to use.

5. Perceiving color, and noting relation to use, as indicating a certain kind of tissue.

6. Analyzing the heart into parts. First, noting possible bases, and then deciding on the basis in light of the foregoing unifying idea — purpose. On this basis, the pupil will arrive at a venous heart and an arterial heart, naming the parts from their function to hold attention to the basis. To name the same parts as right side and left side would be to miss an opportunity. These two parts are again divided on the same basis — as to what each does with the blood it receives. Why the use of the heart requires it to be divided into two parts and then each part into two parts must be considered. This is

purely a matter of thought, and not of perception; and the most complex thought yet required.

The parts are now to be studied in order; each under the attributes and parts which fit it to its function, exactly by the outline of the heart as a whole.

II. *The heart as changing*, in its development from a simple pulsating sack to its permanent form. This point would probably be omitted by the class here supposed; not because of the difficulty of the thought in itself, but because of the obscurity of the facts. Certainly the class would not be able to reach the facts by direct observation; but might picture the stages by means of descriptions from teacher or text. If the pupil can come at the facts, a beautiful narration may be worked out. First, the whole change which the need, or purpose, of the heart brings to pass. Second, the stages in the development, each related to the purpose of the whole change and to every part of the change.

III. *The heart as a symbol of spiritual life.*—Besides the use of the heart to the body it has its use, in a figurative way, to the mind. What this use is, and its adaptation to this use, must be as carefully made out as its physical adaptation to its physical use. At this point the student should make an outline of the attributes and parts of the heart which make it a fit symbol of the spiritual heart—of all that is deepest and best in the soul; such as (1) propelling the life-giving current, (2) being central and vital, (3) rhythmical, etc.

This will illustrate to the reader, again, the point

summed up on page 118, where it was said that "while every individual must be viewed as to how it is at a given moment and how it came to be what it is, it must be made to face both the material and the spiritual world." This last view of the heart is the one in which the mind of the learner most completely finds itself, identifies itself, with the object.

Means to the Steps.— Such a study of the heart as above suggested reveals the method of thought in the heart — reduces it to terms of thought — and thus guides the teacher precisely in stimulating the pupil to create the idea heart. Thus the teacher is prepared to devise means to the steps.

It is needless to give the means to the steps in detail, as the reader can readily supply them from the illustrations in the first chapter. It ought to be emphasized again, however, that such a study of the heart gives the teacher freedom and confidence in the use of means. The conditions of observation and the illustrations to be supplied, and the questions, directions, and suggestions arise at once in the teacher's mind on a consciousness of the mental step required. A teacher thus prepared is free from the text in the recitation, not having to follow questions at bottom of page, and to look at page to see if the answer is correctly given; nor to call on pupils mechanically to recite from side heading in text — the convenient grind of a so-called topical method. Facing the class, free from book or other barrier between teacher and pupil, the teacher can command with precision and force the full and methodical activity of the class throughout the lesson. This at once awakens respect for the skill and power of the teacher, and a feeling of safety in his guidance.

The Value of the Lesson.—Briefly as to its characteristic features only.

1. *Intellectual value.*— As knowledge, the heart serves in mastering myriads of analogous objects; it is an instrument of thought by which the mind comes into unity with the world of thought; and gains its freedom through that unity.

As discipline, the mind is trained to accurate, thorough, and methodical observation, an essential habit in coming into unity with the objective world. The mind is thrown into a universal form of activity in its effort to know this particular object. Especially valuable is that part of the exercise in relating attributes and parts to the purpose of the whole. This organism, while simple and definitely bounded, requires the same form of thought as that necessary to think the whole body, the earth, or the universe. Such is a universal aim which the teacher must hold in consciousness in giving the lesson. The teacher should be conscious in this lesson of helping the pupil to realize in himself a form of activity which is essential to the life of thought. How much must it add to the teacher's pride and joy to feel that this one universal good of life is being realized!

In thus thinking the heart the pupil is trained to follow the lead of the thought in the object considered; or, what is the same thing, he guides his own thought, instead of being passive to the leading of text or teacher. He knows what to think, the order of thinking, and when the object is completely thought. It ought to be said here that if the teacher mechanically applies an outline to an object he will not train the pupil to the power of self-guidance and to the independence of thought required. The pupil must see the relations as determined by the object itself, and not apply a remembered outline. A pupil trained to self-guidance through the object can recite topically and continuously without constant prompting from the teacher, or without a dead tug of memory to bring up the form on the page. He cannot be thrown off the track by interruptions and cross questions from the teacher. Thus to give a pupil freedom in thought is to realize in him one end for which the school exists. The teacher has no right to present the lesson under consideration without being conscious of this phase of its universal value to the pupil.

2. *Emotional and ethical value.* — The emotions are quickened through the perception of the organic unity of the heart. Wonder is aroused in the thought of its perpetual activity; and the æsthetic feeling is aroused in beholding the throbbing physical organ as a type of the throbbing spiritual organ, that other heart of man and of humanity. The figurative use of the heart should be made to stand for much. Every person feeling himself to be "a circulating venous-arterial Heart" in the social system must have a deep sense of moral obligation; and

feeling that within him is a central spiritual force out of which are the issues of life, he must be inclined to consult the inner oracle rather than the sirens along life's pathway. Incidental ethical lessons following in the natural movement of thought have more power than ethical lessons directly given.

APPLICATION III. — DIGESTION.

Take now an example in which the changes are most prominent and easily studied; as in *digestion*. Briefly, it stands thus: —

Purpose, to convert solid to liquid food. Unity of thought requires the attention to rest primarily on the food as changing, and not on the organs by which it is changed. The two series of changes run parallel, but must be kept distinct and in this organic relation — the organs as causing the changes in the food.

1. *Cause* of the changes, mechanical and chemical action. The agents of both named in general.
2. *Time* required to complete the process.
3. *Place* — Alimentary canal described, in general.
4. *Stages of the process.*
    a. Pulverizing the food.
        (1) Purpose, (2) Place — mouth, described and related as means.
    b. Changing Albuminous food to a liquid.
        (1) Purpose, (2) Time, (3) Place — stomach, described and related as a chemical means, aided by mechanical action.

c. Changing Oleaginous and Sugar food to liquid.
 (1) Purpose, (2) Time, (3) Place — described with organs and fluids causing the change.

The foregoing suggests the manner of keeping the action of the organs which serve as means subordinate to the changes in the food. The transition of the food from one place to another should not be mingled with the changes in the nature of the food itself.

APPLICATION IV. — A BATTLE.

A further illustration with an individual viewed wholly as changing — Battle of Concord and Lexington: —

Purpose. — British, to secure supplies; Americans, to defend.

1. *Place* — Lexington, Concord, and on the road from Boston to Concord. (Relation to purpose?)
2. *Time* — 18th of April, 1775; from midnight till afternoon of 19th. (Relation to purpose and condition?)
3. *Cause* — The desirability of holding the supplies. (Relation to purpose?)
4. *Parts* — a. { March of the British from Boston to Lexington. (Relation to main purpose?) Arousing the Minute Men, simultaneous with the above.
    (1) Purpose on the part of the British to reach point by surprise; on the part of the Americans, to defeat their purpose.
    (2) Place — description of (a) route of British, (b) of American territory alarmed.
    (3) Cause — British, advantage via Lexington; Americans, news of intended surprise.

(4) Parts — (a) the secret preparation of the British, the rowing to Charlestown shore, etc.; (b) the ride of Revere and Dawes.

(5) Effects — the fight at Lexington.

b. The battle of Lexington — treated as " a."
c. The march to Concord, with simultaneous events on the part of the Americans — as " a."
d. The retreat — treated as " a."

5. *Effects* — Defeat of British; Americans encouraged.

All the attributes and parts of the foregoing event are unified to thought under its purpose; and unified to the imagination by giving the space and time boundaries of the whole. Unity is further secured by following strictly the order of changes, and by organizing each change into the whole. The relations of the whole define the whole, and the subordinate parts are shown in their subordinate relations.

The foregoing outline contemplates fixing the battle in mind as a mere individual object — a picture object, having certain internal relations and immediate connection with its environment. The imagination, judgment, and the emotions of excitement, fear, courage, and patriotism, are the faculties necessary to form the individual. The picture should be made as full and vivid as life, so that all the emotions will be aroused as intensely as they were in the colonists. The reading of " Paul Revere's Ride " aids in the emotional interpretation.

The battle thus given in its individuality is to be filled with as much universal content through cause and effect, and purpose, as the ability of the class permits. Certainly, they can press the preceding parts of the Revolution into it, and forecast something of the future. This battle will await a higher class for fuller meaning; a class able to comprehend that here was "fired the shot heard round the world."

In this example the emotions are absolutely essential to a knowledge of the battle. Before it is possible to understand the battle the pupil must enter into the feelings aroused, by means of imaginative sympathy. This fact cannot appear in the stiff outline, for it is the glow and flame arising along the whole outline. The same might be said of the will; for the pupil must resolve and make sympathetic effort with those engaged. In short, he must completely indentify himself with the thought, passion, and resolution of the time. Here is one case in which there can be no question as to the pupil's ability to identify himself, to some extent, at least, with the object he studies. And in this union the educational value appears. Besides the value in many other ways, the pupil has an inner resource of life to the extent to which he has made the heroic life of the times his own. To the pupil who has fought the battle sternly it stands as an ever ready suggestion of heroic endeavor in behalf of truth and freedom.

APPLICATION V. — COMPOSITION.

The relations involved in thinking the individual under its two phases of fixed and changing are the guide to the teacher in training the pupils to write descriptions and narrations, two of the four processes involved in composition work. When the pupil is studying the heart or digestion, he may be required to embody his thoughts in good language form. This plan requires him to write under the impulse of the object, and not merely to write for the sake of having an essay for a stated occasion. The fundamental defect of the present system of teaching composition is that of locating the pupil's motive in the wrong phase of the process of composing. His conscious effort is in the form. To him, to compose is to put words together into sentences, sentences together into paragraphs, and paragraphs into discourse. He aims to reach the thought and spirit of his discourse by attention to the form, rather than to secure a perfect form through the spirit. The pupil must be trained to write from the inside out, and not from the outside in. The motive in the writing must be a desire to communicate some idea for the sake of the idea, and not for the sake of the form in which the idea is put. Believe me, the whole matter of school composition would be revolutionized by causing some idea to press for utterance rather than to make the formal requirement for a composition at a fixed time, and merely to test on the formalities of essay writing. In the natural movement of studying the heart, for instance, the pupil will be under the necessity of formulating his thought for the sake of the thought; and his work may be tested in every particular of style. But the impulse shaping every feature of the essay, paragraphing, punctuation, figures of speech, etc., is the heart itself. Thus the teacher gets more thorough and systematic study of the heart than without the essay; and much better training in composition than can be secured by requiring the essay for the sake of the essay. A pupil is not being properly trained to compose unless he is being made conscious that paragraphs, long and short sentences, simple and complex ones, punctuation marks, etc., are all in the object about which he is writing. The comma is in the heart and not in the book of rules.

Suppose pupils are studying a lead pencil, as it now is, and find in it relations about as follows: —

I. As a Whole.
 1. Purpose — to write with.
 2. Position — on the table, not necessary to its use, but to give the mind a picture.
 3. Form — cylindrical. Relation to use.
 4. *Size* — $\begin{cases} \text{Length.} \\ \text{Diameter.} \end{cases}$ Relation to use.
 5. Resistance — light, firm, and strong. Relation to use.
 6. Color — red, not necessary to use, but in a description aids the mind in picturing this pencil.

II. As made up of Parts — basis of functions.
 1. Wood.
  (a) *Purpose* — $\begin{cases} \text{To protect the lead.} \\ \text{To protect fingers from lead.} \\ \text{To give proper size to hold to.} \end{cases}$
  (b) Position — outside of lead. Why?
  (c) Form — hollow cylinder. Why?
  (d) Size — already given, except deducting hollow.
  (e) Resistance — light, firm, and strong. Why?
 2. Lead.
  (a) Purpose — to make the mark.
  (b) Position — inside the wood. Why?

(c) Form — cylindrical. Why?

(d) *Size* — $\begin{cases} \text{Diameter.} \\ \text{Length.} \end{cases}$ Relation to use.

(e) Resistance. — Friable. Relation to use. This attribute is the one through which the pencil's purpose is immediately realized; the attribute that requires the wood, with its attributes.

With such a study as the above, the pupil is ready to make a good oral discourse. He can stand and talk fluently, accurately, methodically, and completely. And completely means that he would know when he was at the end of what he had to say — no small merit in discourse makers. Suppose now the teacher wishes to drill pupils in the form of written discourse. To begin with, the paragraphs are already determined: one for the pencil as a whole, one subdividing it into parts, and one for the wood and one for the lead. These paragraphs are found in the pencil itself. This is a better lesson on paragraphing than to require pupils to put a given page of sentences into paragraphs. In this exercise there is involved the matter of transforming sentences — compound to complex, and then to simple, or the reverse. Sometimes, in books of composition, sentences are given to be transformed as an exercise in securing flexibility of language. But here is a better opportunity. The pupil in following the outline will, perhaps, have these two sentences, or similar ones: "The pencil is to write with. It is on the table." He can readily see that the second sentence states a fact too unimportant to have a separate existence, coördinate with the preceding. The fact of the pencil's position is purely accidental; not aiding the pencil in its purpose, but only giving definiteness to the idea. Then he will revise: "The pencil is to write with, and is on the table." But he can soon be driven to, "The pencil, which is on the table, is to write with." And finally to, "The pencil on the table is to write with"; thus giving the greatest possible subordination to the pencil's position which the structure of the sentence permits. This transformation is required by the relations in the object itself, and is not merely sleight of hand with words.

Note again how variety of sentences and punctuation inhere in the object. After the foregoing sentence the pupil may have these: "It is cylindrical in form. It is six inches long. It is a quarter of an inch in diameter." This chopped-up style is not only unpleasant to the ear but untrue to the thing. The two sentences bearing on the size may be thrown together, since they state parts of the same relation. "The pencil is six inches long, and a quarter of an inch in diameter." There may be reasons for joining this with the preceding. Thus: "The pencil is cylindrical in form, and six inches long and a quarter of an inch in diameter." Note that the omission of the comma before the second *and* is to indicate that the two facts of size are more immediately related than either with form. The comma after the word *form* is in the pencil itself.

Thus the pupil should be drilled, in every phase of style, to work from the inside out — from the spirit to the letter.

APPLICATION VI. — READING.

Equally serviceable are the laws of thinking the individual when applied to a reading lesson. A piece of literature is an individual, and must be studied as such.

Suppose the lesson be "Skipper Ireson's Ride." Whittier presents the Skipper as changing, hence the selection is narration. The pupils are to describe Whittier's narration.

1. The pupils might first be required to picture vividly the changes: (1) the tarring and the feathering; (2) the ride up the rocky lane; (3) the ride through Marblehead; (4) the ride in the country beyond.

2. The purpose of all these changes is to produce in the skipper a feeling of chagrin and humiliation as a punishment for his hard heart in sailing off and refusing to rescue his fellow-townsmen from a sinking vessel because they bragged of their "catch" of fish.

3. Pupils must now show how perfectly adapted were the means devised to produce chagrin and humiliation. To begin with, he was tarred and feathered; and then drawn by women through the town, with such demonstrations as pupils have already described.

4. Next comes the effect of the enterprise. So well adapted, yet it produced no humiliation. Cause of the failure is found in this : —

> "What to me is this noisy ride?
> What is the shame that clothes the skin
> To the nameless horrors that live within?

> Waking or sleeping, I see a wreck,
> And hear a cry from a reeling deck!
> Hate me and curse me, — I only dread
> The hand of God and the face of the dead!"

5. Hence, we must revise the purpose as stated above. The women of Marblehead planned it to produce humiliation; but Whittier's purpose, the poem's purpose, is to make the reader feel how much greater should be the horror of sin in the heart than external shame. This is the purpose which controls the poem.

The foregoing is not the logical order of the analysis, but the chronological, the easiest order of approach for the class. They should now reconstruct, stating clearly the purpose of the poem, and then showing how each attribute and part furthers the purpose. The poem is to present to the reader an ideal sense of sin. Not how we do feel, but how we should feel; how the inner voice cries out in wrong doing. This feeling is thrown out by making it stronger than the worse external forms of shame to which all are extremely sensitive.

The real change will now appear to the student to be the inner change from the hard heart of sin to the penitent heart; and not the external series before sketched. The external series are subordinate, and serve by comparison to bring out the internal. This double series is usually found in a narrative piece of literature; but while the student must approach the inner through the outer, he must face about and state the series of steps as an inner series, showing the relation of the external to it.

The pupil will have no difficulty here of reaching universal, ideal truth — of finding himself. If it seems strange to say that the pupil can identify himself with a river, it certainly will not seem strange to say that he can identify himself with a poem. The poem is a bit of the writer's experience — nothing more; and the student is to reproduce in himself the same experience. The problem of the teacher is how to bring the author and the pupil into unity by means of the poem. The process of such unity is method in teaching reading.

To enforce the application of the doctrine of universal method to reading, one more illustration may be permitted; using a selection quite different in character — Lowell's description of a day in June : —

> " And what is so rare as a day in June?
>   Then, if ever, come perfect days;
> Then Heaven tries the earth if it be in tune,
>   And over it softly her warm ear lays:
> Whether we look, or whether we listen,
> We hear life murmur, or see it glisten;
> Every clod feels a stir of might,
>   An instinct within it that reaches and towers,
> And, groping blindly above it for light,
>   Climbs to a soul in grass and flowers;
> The flush of life may well be seen
>   Thrilling back over hills and valleys;
> The cowslip startles in meadows green,
>   The buttercup catches the sun in its chalice,
> And there's never a leaf or a blade too mean
>   To be some happy creature's palace;

> The little bird sits at his door in the sun,
>   Atilt like a blossom among the leaves,
> And lets his illumined being o'errun
>   With the deluge of summer it receives;
> His mate feels the eggs beneath her wings,
> And the heart in her dumb breast flutters and sings;
> He sings to the wide world, and she to her nest,—
> In the nice ear of Nature which song is the best?"

This poem is an individual, and will be treated as a fixed individual, and not under the influences that prompted it and the steps by which it came to be. Hence, we are to describe Lowell's description; since he is presenting the day at a given time.

I. *Purpose.*—The fundamental attribute of every piece of literature is that of purpose. The writer sets up an ideal experience which he desires to produce in the reader. The discourse is a means the writer uses to make the ideal experience he sets up real in the reader. Therefore, every poem must be studied under one relation—that of purpose and means. After finding the purpose there must be noted the attributes of the poem which make it effective to the end sought.

The purpose of the poem to the reader is the effect produced on the reader. So that a pupil searches for the use of a poem by the process of introspection. He reads and finds in himself an experience. Then, by the analytic judgment he notes the elements of his experience—intellectual, emotional, volitional. Lastly, he decides which of these chiefly occupy consciousness; the others becoming means to the primary one. This effect should again be narrowed to the particular thought, or feeling, or choice.

All readers of the foregoing poem would testify that the burden of experience is emotional. It does not convey knowledge, or stimulate to some particular action. Therefore, as to purpose, or effect produced, this selection is a poem.

This effect must be narrowed from the broad field of emotions to the emotion here awakened. When the reader has decided that the selection is adapted to produce feeling, he then must ask himself how he feels. In this case he will be apt to say that he feels the joy arising from the purity, fullness, and intensity of spiritual life. It is the ecstasy of the overplus of life. The heart beats full and strong, and life is filled to the brim.

This is a highly idealized experience of life. It is the ecstasy not usually felt; a feeling far above the ordinary level of life; the elevation given by the writer's imaginative sentiment wrought to the inspiration point.

II. *Means.* — The foregoing feeling is awakened by the description of a day in June. The new and more exalted experience of life grows out of a new and exalted experience of the June day. The same feeling in a mild degree is awakened by an actual June day; but the feeling here is so heightened as to make it a new experience. The poem makes us feel as we ought to feel in a day in June. This new feeling is produced by a new conception of the June day. This new conception is the most important means to the author's purpose. Let us analyze the conception.

1. Lowell gives but one attribute of the June day, its purpose, perfect adaptation to its work — expressed in the first four lines. Note the words "rare," "perfect," "in tune." The purpose of a day is to bring forth life. It is perfect in proportion as it does this. It is "in tune" if it makes the music of life. This is the beauty of the day which the poem brings out. So far we have nothing but a common view of the day. Closer reading shows that Lowell makes his day not only a power unto physical life, but unto spiritual life. He seeks to make the reader feel the power of the day unto righteousness. This attribute of the day organizes his description. This day has another use than to make corn grow.

2. Lowell makes the reader feel the power of the day by presenting it as a cause producing unusual effect on a wide range of typical objects. For instance: —

a. Causes the clod to *feel* a stir of might; to *reach* and *tower; grope* for light, and *climb* to a *soul*. The day has the power to give human attributes to a clod. In this way the reader is made to feel a stir of might; to reach and tower; and to climb to a soul.

b. Causes life to *flush* and *thrill* over hills and valleys. Only human life can do this — not the vegetable life which he pictures as reappearing. Thus the reader is made to experience the soul's thrill of quickened life.

c. Causes cowslip to *startle;* a sudden nervous excitement — a delight from the sudden influx of life. The cowslip cannot startle, but the reader can.

d. Causes the buttercup to *catch* the sun in its chalice; a conscious effort not possible to the buttercup, but to man. The soul reaches out after the very source of life.

And so through the poem it will be found that the author brings out the power of the day unto life, by showing its effects on various objects — effects manifested in actions. The author uses purpose, cause and effect, and action; action in the form of self-activity.

It has been suggested that the new and exalted feeling awakened by the poem is accomplished by means of the author's new and exalted conception, which chiefly constitutes his description. The chief thing which makes this description adequate to its purpose is that of transforming the ordinary power of the day unto physical life, making the characteristic figure of the poem personification.

3. Subordinate to the foregoing, and as a means to it, Lowell presents a panorama of landscape which with its color and variety delights the eye and ear, as, the fresh appearance of life over hills and valleys; life murmuring and glistening; the little bird singing at his door in the sun, "atilt like a blossom among the leaves"; leaves and blades, as happy creatures' palaces, etc., — all of the mere picture side of the day.

4. Under sound comes the music of the poem — euphony, harmony, rhythm, rhyme, alliteration, and balanced sentences.

It is not the purpose here to analyze the poem further than to show that the analysis falls into the universal thought movement.

THINKING THE GENERAL.

The Two Phases of the Process. — The distinction between the individual and the general was drawn on pages 109 to 114. The distinction is not in the subject-matter, but in the view taken. In one, the individual in its own organic constitution; in the other, as to its common nature, common origin, with other individuals. Therefore the discussion of the general does not leave out of sight the individual; but gives special emphasis to one relation of it — its general or universal nature. The general is not an abstraction; but is a general only through individuals.

As before stated, the individual is the beginning and the end of knowledge. Dewey says, "What is actually known is always a combination of the universal and the particular; of law and fact; in other words, an individual. The individual known is becoming constantly a richer object of knowledge, by virtue of the two processes of universalization and definition. The individual known is always becoming more universal, because it is being identified with other individuals, under some common relation or idea. It is becoming more definite, for these various relations which are thus recognized are taken into it, and become part of its content; they enlarge its significance and serve to distinguish it. A completely universalized or related individual, which is at the same time perfectly definite or distinct in all its relations, is, therefore, the end of knowledge."

A part of what is implied in the above applies to the preceding treatment of the individual, in pushing it out into its infinite organic relations. But it serves here to emphasize the thought that while the general notion, or class, is proposed for treatment, it is still the individual in a new relation; not this time, however, the individual as having parts which coöperate, or as being a part coöperating with other individuals, but the individual as to its common idea, origin, nature, with other individuals.

As there are two phases of thinking the individual — as fixed and as changing — so there are two phases of thinking the general, corresponding closely to the two preceding; and depending, also, on the way the subject is viewed. The general idea is formed from individuals by a process of judgment; and it may be applied to the individuals from which it was derived by another form of the same process. The concept considered as to the process of its formation, gives rise to a distinct process of thought called *Exposition*. The concept considered in the process of its application to actually existing things gives rise to a process of thought called *Argumentation*.

We form the general ideas *red* and *men* from red objects and from this and that man. These general ideas exist as such only in the mind that forms them. These general ideas may now be applied to the world of reality, and we find a red object and this and that man. The decision that a given general notion is found in a given individual, or individuals, is the subject-matter of argumentation; while the general notion in itself is the subject-matter of exposition. The general idea is formed from the world as presented in observation, through the processes of comparison and contrast, and abstraction and generalization. How it is formed constitutes the process of exposition. This general notion sprang from the objective world of reality by a process of thought, and tends to return through another process of thought to do service in this same world of reality. A complete study of a general idea requires it to pass through both these movements of thought. If the teacher is treating the general idea Free Trade, he must first develop the notion Free Trade, and then apply the notion to practical life. It takes both views to constitute a knowledge of Free Trade.

Recalling now the universal law of mental movement, it will be readily observed that the two foregoing processes are only phases of that universal movement. The mind moves from the individual to the universal and back to the individual. Exposition seeks the universal; argumentation returns with it to the individual.

Forming the General Notion.

The Two Phases of the Process. — It has already been observed that a general idea, to be general, must contain individuals. The general must be general to something. Every exposition, therefore, is the process of thinking the general in unity with the individual. Emphasizing one of these relations, the common, forms what is known as the *Content* of the general idea; emphasizing the other, the individual, forms the *Extent* of the general idea.

The content of a general idea is the sum of attributes common to a number of individuals. The content of the class quadruped is the sum of the attributes, sensation, voluntary motion, vertebral structure, peculiar nervous and circulatory systems, quadrupedal, and so on, including whatever else may be found in each animal of that class. This content is the sum of the common attributes of a number of objects — such attributes in any object as may be found in every other of the class. The mind, in thinking the content of a class, must, at the same time, think the individuals in which the content finds its concrete being — must think the extent of the class. The extent of a class is the number of individuals in which the content is found. The content of the class red apple is the sum of the common attributes; the extent is the sum of the individuals in the class.

The content of a class determines the extent. One bears an inverse ratio to the other. If the class animal have for its content the sum of the two attributes, sensation and voluntary motion, and a third be added, warm blooded, thus increasing the content, the extent is decreased by dropping from the idea the cold blooded animals. With each addition of a new attribute to the content, there is a subtraction from its extent — a subtraction of the number not having the attribute added.

This brings us to the two phases of thinking necessary to form a general idea; one, that of thinking the content; the other, the extent. The first process is known as *Definition;* the second, as *Division.*

THINKING THE CONTENT OF A CLASS.

Developing definitions is so prominent a part of the teacher's work that the method of it deserves careful attention. Definition is not, in its essential nature, a formal word process; but a mental process of conceiving the content of a class of objects.

This definition of Definition becomes more explicit by observing that the content of a general idea is constituted of two relations — the *universal* and the *particular*, or its likeness to and difference from other ideas.

The class oak tree has a common nature with all trees; through them with organic life; and through organic objects with all being. If the attributes which the oak tree has in common with trees, or with the larger group of organic objects, or with the universe of objects, be taken away, the oak is destroyed. Also, if that which separates the oak tree from the class tree be taken away, the oak is destroyed. The class oak cannot exist except through the union of both phases of this truth. It is the life and being of the class oak tree. Again, imagine before us all apples. These apples have attributes in common. Some of the common attributes are peculiar to apples alone, and the others are found in stones, in oranges, in birds, in man, in everything — are universal. To think away either those that are common and peculiar, or those that are common and universal, is to destroy the thought of apples. The union of the common, particular attributes with the common, universal attributes constitutes the nature of apples.

Therefore, the fundamental truth in any class of things is the truth common to them and to the larger class òf which they are a part, plus the truth common to them alone, and which permanently distinguishes them from the class of things to which they belong. The first phase of the truth maintains the connection of the class with universal being; the second, the particular existence of the class to some definite end.

Since definition is to exhibit the content of an idea, and since this content is the union of the two relations of particular and universal, definition may be explicitly defined as *the process of forming a conception of the universal and the particular nature of an idea.* That is, a definition is a process of forming a conception of the essential nature of the idea under discussion. Hence their necessity and general use.

Therefore, method in definition is the mental process of conceiving in unity the particular and universal nature of a general idea.

The particular element unifies the individuals, and at the same time separates them from all other individuals; while the universal unifies the individuals, and, at the same time, connects the group unified with the universe out of which the individuals spring.

Steps and Laws in the Process.—(1) Since the general is based on the individual, the first step in the process is that of Observation; or rather, observation is continued through as a condition of the other processes; (2) Comparison and Contrast of individuals; (3) Abstraction, in fixing the attention on what is common; (4) Generalization, in applying the common element abstracted to the individuals in order to unify them.

These activities are necessarily involved in grasping the two phases of content. Using the noun to illustrate, let us suppose the student is already supplied with some more comprehensive idea, that of *word*, as expressing an idea. Individual words, including nouns and other words, must be observed, compared, and contrasted until the pupil finds the likeness between the class studied and all other words; namely, that all express ideas; and the difference between the words studied and all other words; namely, that they name objects. This last difference and the former likeness are both common to all nouns, binding them into the unity of the class and the class into the unity of all words, and the universe.

The last generalization may be stated as follows : A noun is a substantive which expresses its object by naming it.

It should be observed that the universal truth is formally presented in definition by referring the class to be defined to a known larger class of which it is a part. Whenever an object or class is said to be in a larger class, however small the larger class, a connection is established with the universe. To say that a noun is a substantive is to say that it is the arbitrary expression of an object, and to say this is to say that it is the arbitrary expression of an idea; which further implies that it, at least, is the expression of an idea. Now this last fact is true of every object in the universe. All express thought. Nothing can be correctly defined without connecting it with the sun, moon, and stars; and the definitions which have power to the student are those in which he can feel his way back to, become conscious of, the universal element. This reference of an idea to a larger whole is only a concise and an abbreviated form of giving the universal.

It follows from what has been said that the larger class to which reference is made must be a known class, and such as will give the clearest and fullest notion of the class defined. Reference is made to the known class to abbreviate the process; and if this class need explanation the purpose is defeated. For the same reason, the class to which reference is made should have the greatest content, and, therefore, the least extent of any class to which reference can be made. Reference is made to the larger class to save enumerating and explaining common attributes of the class defined; and the greater the number found in the larger class the greater is the economy. For instance, in defining a pronoun it may be referred to the class words, or to the smaller class substantives. The choice will be determined, first, by which is better known; second, by which has the greater content. If the substantive has been previously defined, it must be selected; because it contains one more attribute in common with the noun than does the class words. Saying that a noun is a word is saying only that it expresses an idea; but saying that it is a substantive is saying that it expresses an idea of an object.

Thus we arrive at the first law for making a definition: *Present the universal nature of the class by referring it to the smallest known class of which it is a part.*

The next step in the formal definition is the statement of the attribute which gives the class its separate being. In stating this attribute, two points must be observed. Since the attribute now to be stated is that which separates the class from all other objects, care must be taken that the common attribute is not found in any other object; that is, that the definition be not too broad. The second fact is, that since the attribute is not only particular but common, care must be taken that it include all the objects over which the generalization extends; that is, that it be not too narrow, and thus divide the class which it was intended to unify.

But the law worthy of the most special attention in giving the particular mark of the class defined is that of unity. If an attribute be given which belongs only to a part of the individuals, and then a second be given to include some of the remainder, and another to include what is left, three classes are given instead of one. For instance, "A verb is a word that expresses action, state, or being." Action does not belong to all verbs; neither does state, nor being. If we should take all verbs in the language and place them before us as the definition requires, we should have three groups instead of one. The attribute must unify; and to do this it must belong to every verb in the language. The violation of unity is, perhaps, the most common and fundamental error in making definitions. It fosters loose and superficial habits of thought, and misses the truth sought.

Thus we arrive at the second law for making a definition: *State the one common, particular attribute of the class,* — that which unifies all the individuals of the class and at the same time separates them from all others.

Educational Value of Definition. — Method in definition has been defined as the process of thinking individuals into unity; or the process of forming the content of a general idea. This was seen to involve the relations of particular and universal — the particular, in unifying, distinguishes the class from others; while the universal, in unifying, connects the class defined with others. By reference again to the ultimate law of method, and the ultimate problem of thought, definition will appear in its true light, and at its true value. It is a process of thinking which brings into unity the individual and universal — the problem of all thought, and which brings the learner into unity with the world of thought, the end of all learning. This is its primary educational value.

The power to discern unity in the midst of diversity; to detect essential likenesses amidst engrossing and non-essential differences; to find the enduring under the mask of obtruding, accidental, and superficial attributes, is a fundamental characteristic of every well-trained mind. To define is not simply to unify individuals; but, in unifying, to find their essential nature. The common nature in which they are unified is the essential nature of each individual. Hence the habit of thinking in the form of definition is the habit of thinking the true nature of things; which is the primary function of mind.

This unifying act of mind is complex ; and has a richer significance in training than at first appears. It requires accurate, thorough, and methodical observation ; precise discrimination through comparison and contrast ; abstraction of that which abides after differences have been canceled ; and generalization, by holding in mind the differences of individuals while binding them into the unity of their common nature. So that while training to correct habits of definition, the teacher is carrying forward a large number of related habits. Too much cannot be said, therefore, by way of urging the teacher to train the student in the power of logical definition ; since it is a form of activity by which he comes into unity with the world of thought.

Definitions are usually treated as mere formal statements to be recited and lodged away in memory, rather than thought processes in fundamental forms of mental activity. That a student have a correct definition of a fraction is itself of little consequence ; but that, in making such a definition, he has gained new power over the process of defining is vital to his education ; and, also, essential to the full truth in the particular thing defined.

To reap the best results, the formal statement of a definition should not be made until the student has had a full experience of all the subordinate processes on which the definition is based. In some cases, days, or even weeks, should be spent in observing, comparing and contrasting, abstracting, and generalizing, before any effort is made to formulate a definition. The formal definition of an infinitive is the last step in the process and not the first, as usually given. A definition made in this way, when asked for in reproduction, will not be remembered as a form of words; but the entire experience in making the definition will, in brief, be repeated. Definitions made in this way cannot be forgotten; or, if forgotten, may be reconstructed on a moment's notice.

THINKING THE EXTENT OF A CLASS.

Definition is the process of thinking diversity into unity; division is the process of thinking unity into diversity. In definition, the mental movement is from the individuals toward the general; in division, from the general towards the individuals. The first is the "upward way" of knowing; the second, the "downward way"; using Plato's words. Each process is necessary to the full meaning of the other; and the two constitute the method in every scientific classification; the one setting forth the content of the class, and the other, the extent. Definition sets forth the unity of the noun by giving its content; connecting it at the same time with the other parts of speech. Division separates this class into the kinds; as concrete and abstract nouns; uniting at the same time the two classes into the class noun. These may again be subdivided into others; and the process thus continued till individuals are reached; connecting at each subdivision the parts into the whole subdivided. By these two movements, we arrive at an organic, unified conception of the noun.

It should be observed that each division has implicit in it a new definition; while each definition involves a division. The two are complementary phases of the same process. The distinction arises in a difference of emphasis by the attention. In definition, the emphasis is given to the unity of the parts; in division, to the parts in unity. The mind cannot think a class without the common content which unifies, and the parts which are unified; so that definition always implies division, and division, definition. When the noun is defined, it must, in its unification, be separated from other parts of speech; and at the same time connected with them; and when the noun is divided into concrete and abstract, the unifying attribute of each class must be given, along with the common attribute which binds the two classes into the noun. A definition of each of these must state the common attribute recognized in the division; and at the same time unify the two in the noun by the attribute used in the division. Thus Definition and Division are not two things, but organic phases of the same mental process.

Steps and Laws in the Process.—From the nature of division, its laws and processes are readily ascertained. The steps are practically the same as in definition. The fundamental law requires that the unity of the class be maintained in the process of division. This means that each sub-class be thought into its own unity, at the same time that all the sub-classes are thought into the unity of the whole. It will be recalled that in definition the common attribute in which the class was unified had two phases, the particular and the universal. The same fact appears in division. The sub-classes must be unified in the whole by some attribute which must extend, at least, to all the individuals of all the sub-classes, while each sub-class has its own particular unifying attribute. The unifying attribute of each part must be some phase of the unifying attribute of the whole class, in order that the sub-classes be united in the class. The individuals in the class noun are unified in the fact that all express objects. Some phase of this fact must serve to unite the parts of the class, and thus to divide it. The basis of both separation and division is that of expression. This fact unifies the parts of the class in the whole. Some nouns are found to express abstract objects, and some concrete. Each of these sub-classes is unified on the same basis — expression. It is illogical in thought and impossible in fact to unify one sub-class on one basis and another on another basis. Make the trial of putting the class apples in bunches; the apples in one bunch being alike in color; of another, in taste; of another, in size, etc.; and it will readily appear why it cannot be done in thought. Thus try to place on the table in groups actual nouns; the nouns in one group being alike in that they express concrete objects; in another, in that they have two syllables, etc. This will make clear what is meant by securing unity in each of the sub-classes respectively, and of all the sub-classes in the whole.

It is a fine exercise, which should be often repeated, for the student to test the unity of his division by placing before him, in imagination at least, the actual objects being classified. This will train him in thought to be true to the relation among things.

The first step, therefore, in securing unity in division is to select some fundamental basis of division, as already determined by the definition of the class to be subdivided. The second is to unify each sub-class on the one basis selected.

As before stated, the attribute of expression is the unifying attribute of the noun, as set forth by its definition: A noun is a word that names an object. This essential fact of the class must be carried through as the basis of division and unity among the sub-classes. In expression, nouns differ as to the *kind* of objects expressed, — some express concrete objects, giving the class concrete nouns; and some, abstract objects, giving rise to abstract nouns. The concrete nouns again differ in expression as to the kind of *concrete* objects expressed; some expressing individuals; some classes; some collections; and some, masses; giving rise to proper nouns, class nouns, collective nouns, and mass nouns. The abstract nouns differ in expression as to the kind of *abstract* object expressed; some expressing qualities, some actions, some conditions, and some relations; giving rise to classes of nouns of the same names.

Educational Value of Division.— One mark of every well-trained mind is the habit of reducing a class into a system of logical subdivisions. This requires accuracy, thoroughness, method, and unity in the mental process. For the sake of the discipline which the mind gains by fitting its thought into the system of things, the student must be held rigidly to the law of unity in logical subdivision. As soon as possible he should be made conscious of the law, that he may guide his own processes. He should never be permitted to make loose systems of classes; for in so doing he is becoming a slave to slovenly habits of thought. The practice of the teacher is sadly at fault at this point. Any sort of loose jumble of parts is tolerated. The pupil copies the classes given in the text without concern as to the process by which they are constituted. Whether the outline is right or wrong matters little; the error is in the passive reception of it. The pupil should either construct his own outline, or test the one given so as to make it his own. It is not the fact of having the outline, but the fact of performing the process by which the outline is produced that gives it value. The thing needed is the form of mental activity to which the mind is trained—a form essential to unity with the world's thought.

THE PROCESSES MOVING IN UNITY.

Let us now observe the two processes of definition and division moving in unity, the better to note their method and significance. Suppose the student has risen to the point in his grammar work where he is to treat systematically Parts of Speech. He has analyzed sentences until arriving at the conclusion that the organic parts of the sentence are words, phrases, and clauses. He has now the idea of words as Parts of Speech, *i.e.*, of words as expressing ideas organized in a thought.

Let us suppose then that the pupil has before him the multitude of words in the language, bound together by the one attribute of expressing organic parts of a thought. This conception, reached by a long course of sentence analysis, is his starting point in studying parts of speech. Prepared with this one conception, he is to begin his study with the multitude of individual words as found in sentences before him. With these individual words he begins, and with them, too, he closes — from individuals to individuals by successive alternations of definitions and divisions, based on comparison and contrast of individual words.

Having defined parts of speech from his experience with words in analyzing sentences, his next step is to subdivide them. The definition fixed the attention on the common attribute of the class. This common attribute is the basis on which the division is to be made. At the same time the student defines he establishes the basis for his subdivision. The common attribute is that of expressing the organic elements of a thought. The difference must be found in the expression of the organic elements. The pupil now begins a new course of observation and comparison and contrast to find this time the differences which may coexist with the likeness expressed in the definition. The differences are the new likenesses binding into unity the sub-classes. The pupil will readily note the broad distinction between those words which express ideas in the thought and those which express relations between the ideas — *idea* words and *relation* words. This is the fundamental distinction, for thought consists of ideas in relation. This division implies the definition of idea word and relation word, and these are readily formulated by the student.

For brevity of illustration, let relation words be dropped. Next comes the subdivision of idea words. Again the student with sentences before him compares and contrasts idea words to find the broadest distinction running through them. The basis of division is the attribute expressed in the definition; the attribute which unifies the class idea-words must itself be the dividing principle. The likeness is the expression of ideas; the difference must be found in the expression of ideas. A few days' search with careful discrimination will reveal to the pupil the next broadest distinction among parts of speech — the expression of objects, or those ideas which may serve as the subjects of thought; and the expression of attributes, or those ideas which serve as predicates of thought. At the same time this distinction is being discovered, the new likeness arises in mind; the difference between attributive words and substantive words cannot be discovered without discovering at the same time the likeness among attributive words and substantive words. Hence the development of the division of the larger class is the development of the definitions of each of the classes made by the subdivision.

Again for brevity let substantives be dropped. The pupil now being supplied with sentences containing all kinds of attributive words, is directed, suppose for the first lesson, to write out the likenesses and differences between the following words in the sentence, "The timely suggestion was kindly received": *timely* and *kindly; timely* and *was received; kindly* and *was received.* In class he reads the result of his thinking; and many others are compared and contrasted orally. The process is continued a few days, till all possible varieties of attributive words have been included. These conclusions will force themselves on the pupil: Some attributive words express attributes of objects; some express attributes of objects and assert the attribute of the object; others express attributes of attributes, or express attributes of objects indirectly; while the first mentioned express attributes of objects directly. The names adjective, adverb, and attributive verb now being given, the pupil will properly define each class.

Following now only the adjective, the pupil, supplied with all varieties in sentences, is by study as before to discover the broadest distinction; that between predicate and modifying adjective; the first universalizing its object, and the second particularizing it. To say that this paper is white is to universalize it by connecting it with all white things; to say white paper is to particularize it, separate it from other paper. Following out modifying adjectives by the same method of discovery, the many subtle ways in which modifications are made must be noted. The most fundamental is that in which the modification is made in the content only or in the extent — descriptive and limiting adjectives. Limiting adjectives make their limitations in various ways ; as, ten horses, and white horses. The attribute ten is not found in each horse but in the group taken as a whole ; but the attribute white is found in each horse ; and limits by classifying, as the other limits by quantifying.

Similarly moving on all the lines as hinted here, a few stages bring the student to individual words, such as I, London, bright, etc.; the same words with which he began his search. Then what does this movement in a circle signify ? It means primarily that the words have a richer content. At each of the five or six stages of definition and division an attribute is added to each word, giving a meaning five or six times as full as at the outset. In this process, too, the words are universalized and definitely individualized ; which is the end of knowledge. The pupil has descended from the universal truth that all objects express ideas, to words as arbitrary symbols expressing ideas ; down to words expressing ideas, in a restricted sense, and relations ; and so on, carrying the universal meaning downward with every division. And in every definition the individual is thrown back on the universal. Thus when the individual is reached at the end of the process, it is completely universalized. And, too, it is definitely individualized, for at each successive division narrower attributes were given ; and this continued till the division reached the individual word. Definition, also, enforces the individualizing attributes of the object; for every definition, as already observed, states both the particular and the universal attributes of the object. As the successive definitions defined successively smaller classes there comes a point at last at which the strictly individualizing attribute must be stated. Such then is the significance of this double movement, making perfectly distinct and universal the individual.

From another point of view, words become organized and systemized into knowledge. The process brings into view the greatest possible variety in the subject matter; but at the same time, it brings it into the closest unity. The greater the diversity in unity the richer, fuller, and more accurate the knowledge. The common attributes of the objects studied must be brought out; but with them there must be developed the greatest possible diversity.

Thus again we return through the special laws of Definition and Division to the universal law of method.

EXPOSITION OF IDEAL TRUTH.

So far in the discussion reference has been had to matter-of-fact truth; truth conceived by the logical processes of the judgment — observation, comparison and contrast, and generalization; generalization first to the extent of observation, and second beyond observation by means of induction. In conceiving ideal truth the creative imagination takes the place of the logical judgment, converting the real into the ideal.

In matter-of-fact truth the mind strives to adjust itself accurately to the external object; in ideal truth the mind constructs the object according to the inner law of the mind itself. The merit of a scientific treatment is the accuracy and faithfulness with which the mind conforms to the truth as it actually exists; but in a poetic treatment the merit consists in the perfection with which the ideal is illuminated where only dimly shadowed forth in the real. The imagination, in its passion for the perfect, penetrates the object and satisfies itself by adding, subtracting, and rearranging the elements until it contemplates the perfect. The mind craves to behold an ideal river, mountain, landscape, or character; and not finding them, makes them according to its own type.

When Wordsworth says that the sunshine is a glorious birth, he does not speak the truth of the scientific judgment concerning sunshine, but of how the mind in an idealized and exalted mood would have it. Longfellow takes the same liberty with daybreak in the following: —

> A wind came up out of the sea,
> And said, "O mists, make room for me."
> It hailed the ships, and cried, "Sail on,
> Ye mariners, the night is gone."
> And hurried landward far away,
> Crying, "Awake! it is the day."
> It said unto the forest, "Shout!
> Hang all your leafy banners out!"
> It touched the wood-bird's folded wing,
> And said, "O bird, awake and sing."

> And o'er the farms, "O chanticleer,
> Your clarion blow; the day is near."
> It whispered to the fields of corn,
> "Bow down, and hail the coming morn."
> It shouted through the belfry-tower,
> "Awake, O bell! proclaim the hour."
> It crossed the churchyard with a sigh,
> And said, "Not yet! in quiet lie."

This daybreak is in the mind, discerned only by the inner eye, and cannot be discovered by the outer organ. The wind does not go forth and hail the ships, and call upon the forest to shout and wave its banners in joy at the coming day; does not touch the wood-bird's folded wing to call forth a morning song; nor command the corn to bow down in worship in honor of the approaching sovereign. But the mind, born into new life, thus goes forth; shouts and sings; bows down and hails with reverence the advent of the coming day. The imagination creates a daybreak to suit its own ideal way of feeling about it; a more exalted feeling than accompanies our ordinary experience.

This ideal truth falls within the scope of human life; and is further narrowed in being what the soul aspires to, rather than what it has attained. The ideal is the soul's consciousness of its possibilities, and is thus the measure of what man may attain, and what he strives to attain; but it is to him not a matter of fact, but only of idea. History and literature express the two sides of human life — the real and the ideal. History reveals the struggle of the race to attain its ideal; literature sets up in advance the goal to which the race aspires, and urges the reader to higher and nobler attainment.

The logical processes of exposition deal with all kinds of general truth; but the ideal truth of human life has also the special province of fine art; and, so far as our purpose here goes, it falls to reading and literature studies. The author of a poem or a novel exhibits the ideal working of some law of human life. It is universal truth he seeks; something fundamental and essential in life; but the method is quite different from the logical method of exposition. Instead of the processes of the judgment we have the imagination creating the truth to be set forth, and also the concrete individual in which the truth is exhibited. In the logical process there is generalization from individuals; some general truth is abstracted; but in the poetic process there is no abstracting; there is concreting. The ideal, or type, arises first in the mind, and a single individual is created to embody it. In the other case, individuals exist first, and the type is sought by the processes of judgment. The general truth in a piece of literature is adequately embodied in a single object. We have here the immediate unity of the individual and universal. The individual must be adequate to the universal; there must be no conflict between the two. Everywhere the universal strives to realize itself in the individual; this is its nature; but it becomes distorted in the process. The imagination creates the object so as to give the universal its freedom. The universal idea patriotism is compressed when found in individual men; but the poet portrays a man who gives patriotism free scope. Charity is a universal law of human spirit — its universal and essential nature; but as we find it in this person and in that it is cramped in a narrow mind or dissolved in selfishness. But Lowell gives us a type in the " Vision of Sir Launfal " through which universal charity flows without obstruction. This is the harmony between the individual and the universal, between the sense and the reason, which gives rise to the æsthetic feeling. We pronounce a thing beautiful on feeling that the idea in it has free manifestation. The problem for the one who proposes this method of setting forth universal truth is to present to the senses or to the imagination an individual which expresses freely the idea sought. In architecture, sculpture, and painting, the individual is presented to the senses; in music and literature to the imagination, thus freeing the individual from the grossness of matter.

This brief statement gives the key to reading and literature work, in showing that the pupil's attention must move along three fundamental lines : —

1. He must search out, state, and explain the ideal content in terms of human life;

2. Must form fully and vividly the image through which the universal shines forth;

3. Must show wherein the individual pictured is in harmony with the universal idea.

The reading lesson was touched upon in treating the individual, since a piece of discourse is an individual. But its true nature now appears much more fully; for every reading lesson, being a piece of literature, expresses some universal truth of life in the form of some individual object. A brief application of the foregoing doctrine to a reading lesson will now show the deeper method of treatment. Suppose the lesson to be on —

EXCELSIOR.

The shades of night were falling fast,
As through an Alpine village passed
A youth who bore, 'mid snow and ice,
A banner with the strange device,
    Excelsior !

His brow was sad ; his eye beneath
Flashed like a falchion from its sheath,
And like a silver clarion rung
The accents of that unknown tongue,
    Excelsior !

In happy homes he saw the light
Of household fires gleam warm and bright ;
Above, the spectral glaciers shone,
And from his lips escaped a groan,
    Excelsior !

"Try not the Pass !" the old man said ;
"Dark lowers the tempest overhead,
  The roaring torrent is deep and wide !"
And loud that clarion voice replied,
    Excelsior !

"O stay," the maiden said, "and rest
  Thy weary head upon this breast !"
A tear stood in his bright blue eye,
But still he answered with a sigh,
    Excelsior !

"Beware the pinetree's withered branch!
Beware the awful avalanche!"
This was the peasant's last Good-night,
A voice replied, far up the height,
    Excelsior!

At break of day, as heavenward
The pious monks of Saint Bernard
Uttered the oft-repeated prayer,
A voice cried through the startled air,
    Excelsior!

A traveller, by the faithful hound,
Half-buried in the snow was found,
Still grasping in his hand of ice
That banner with the strange device,
    Excelsior!

There in the twilight cold and gray,
Lifeless, but beautiful, he lay,
And from the sky, serene and far,
A voice fell, like a falling star,
    Excelsior!

We have seen that pupils must take three steps: (1) picture the individual; (2) conceive the universal — the theme; (3) note the fitness of the individual to body forth the universal.

1. Suppose that pupils be required to draw, in clear outline and in vivid colors, the picture here presented. They must note the unity of the picture in the physical act of the youth: it is the picture of a physical act of climbing the Alps at a given time under insurmountable difficulties — the darkness, the storm, the spectral glacier,

the avalanche, the tempest, the roaring torrent; and against special allurements of the gleaming household fires and the maiden's invitation to stay and rest. The banner must be noted, the earnest brow, the flashing eye, the clarion voice with its constant cry of "excelsior" in spite of allurements and dangers. The pupils must see in this physical act a daring and hopeless attempt, yet unwavering even unto death.

2. Next, let the pupils be pressed for the significance of the picture; whether it is given for the sake of the physical act, or for something else. The picture alone has value to the emotions; awakens a feeling of awe, sublimity, and physical courage. But this would give little meaning worthy of a piece of literature. It may be thought a warning against fool-hardy attempts. Some one criticizes Longfellow severely for giving us here nothing better than a crank for a hero. But there are many indications that Longfellow meant something better than the critic discerned. The banner, with its strange device, the flashing eye, the clarion voice, beautiful in death, and especially the voice from heaven like a falling star — all indicate some meaning above physical courage or fool-hardiness. If such courage is all, the critic is right; and the poem has no message to man.

But if the reader will look through this daring and unwavering physical act, to a daring and unwavering spiritual act to which the lines hint and the heart feels in reading, the fool-hardy crank disappears and the spiritual hero emerges. What is it to climb the Alps? It is to strive for the highest good of the soul in spite of ease, allurements, and threatening dangers. This physical act is a type of the spiritual act of striving for the unattainable ideal. To climb the Alps is to stand by principle even in the face of death; to abide by the true self against all allurements and in face of all dangers. While it may be questionable courage to climb the Alps under such circumstances, it is not so in climbing the heights of moral sublimity. We give all honor to the man who is a martyr to a principle; or to the one who unwaveringly and without debate moves resolutely onward to the goal of noble manhood or womanhood.

Such is the ideal spiritual truth which is mirrored forth by the physical act of the youth in climbing the Alps. It is ideal because it is the way all should strive; and it is universal because this ideal urgency finds a response in every heart. It is a universal ideal. It ought to be noted also that it is universal in the sense of being fundamental and essential in the development of the soul. It touches life from its center to its circumference, coloring all its sentiments and controlling all its actions. The poem is, therefore, of high grade, so far as the quality of the theme is concerned.

3. In the next step the pupil must show how the individual physical act is an adequate expression of the ideal, universal truth. First, the physical act was so difficult as to require the sacrifice of life. If it had been an ordinary affair of strolling up an undulating mountain-side, it would have been no test of physical

courage, and no type of that moral courage which holds on to the good of the soul against every counter force. If Longfellow had pictured such a physical feat he would not have represented the heroism of the soul in facing physical death for spiritual life.

The physical act is given the more intensity by thrusting aside, as well as dangers in the pathway, the temptations of ease and allurements — the gleaming of household fires amidst the snow and ice, and the maiden's entreaty. By thus giving the picture the two parts of dangers and allurements, the writer typifies the two classes of forces that turn man from seeking his ideal. Bringing the two together makes it doubly strong. Man is turned from his ideal either by the love of ease and the seductions of life, or by trials and dangers confronting him.

The difficulty and danger of climbing the Alps is made alarming by the darkness, the snow and ice, the tempest, the roaring torrent, the spectral glacier, and the awful avalanche. With such dangers and allurements it must be noted that it did not occur to the youth to debate the question of moving upward. With sad, earnest brow and flashing eye, his clarion voice rang forth the motto of his life, without stopping to reply to the maiden's entreaty or the old man's or the peasant's warning. Without this steadiness and persistency in the physical act, it would not express the ideal holding after the good of the soul.

It must be noted that the ideal character of the theme is well expressed by the choice of the poet's words in describing the physical act. In speaking of the banner he says it was a "strange device," "an unknown tongue." Also, that the air was "startled" by the voice uttering the motto. This was not an unknown tongue because it was Latin; but because it was not the customary motto on the banner of life. It is a strange thing to find a young man moving through life completely under the control of the highest ideal. If there had been inscribed on the banner, business, money, thrift, success in "getting on," the air would not have been startled and the device would not have been strange. All can speak that tongue. Any young man in a community who devotes himself wholly to the soul's chief good will speak an unknown tongue to those about him. His banner would be strange among banners in the mad rush of the business world. To suit that community the poem would have to be rewritten after this style:—

> The shades of night were falling fast,
> As through an Alpine village passed
> A youth, who bore 'mid snow and ice,
> A banner with the *familiar* device,
>   *Money!*

Finally, he was beautiful in death; and "still grasping in his hand of ice the banner with the strange device," showing that he grasped firmly his ideal even in death. But the climax of embodiment is reached when "from the sky serene and far, a voice fell like a falling star,"—the heavenly witness of triumph where the world can see but failure. If the teacher wishes to press this lesson on the side of oral expression he will have only to note that oral expression in all of its qualities is determined by the relation of the embodiment to the theme, — in fact is but the oral form of the embodiment.

There is here no space for further illustrations; but if the teacher will pursue this thought diligently he will find that, while there are infinite variations, the thought of the student must move along the lines above suggested.

Applying the General Notion.

It has already been stated that the general notion may be considered, not only in its nature and process of formation, but in its application to concrete reality and life. It is one thing to form the concept plant or democratic government, and another thing to use these concepts to increase knowledge and to guide conduct. As already stated, the general notion is applied by a process called Argumentation. The process is based on the organic relation of the individual, particular, and universal. It will facilitate the discussion to make clear at the outset the relation of these ideas.

Under exposition it was shown that the general idea is formed from individual objects by binding them into unity among themselves, and at the same time binding this unity into the unity of the universe. Thus the general idea has its universal and particular relations in unity with individual objects.

Particular attributes are those common to all the individuals of the class, but not extending to any individual beyond the class; thus binding the individuals of the class into their own unity. Universal attributes are also common to the individuals of the class, but they extend beyond the class, binding it into some larger unity with other classes. The individual, as well as the class, has attributes which extend beyond it; these are also called universal. Universal is here used in the sense that the attribute extends beyond the individual or the class under consideration. The mind consciously puts a limit to individual and particular attributes; but universal attributes are not limited in thought. When it is said that a noun expresses an object by naming it, the particular mark, "by naming it," has definite limit given to it in thought; it terminates in the last noun, and the thinker is conscious of the fact. But the universal attribute, "expressing an object," connects the noun with the pronoun, and with various other things expressing objects, not at the time definitely limited in thought. The universal attribute may connect the class defined only with the immediate larger class; but it is still universal, for this larger class has connections out through larger and still larger classes till the universe is reached. Any attribute which connects the class under consideration with any larger class is called a universal attribute.

Argumentation is a peculiar movement of the mind from the individual through the particular to the universal; and from the universal through the particular to the individual. It thus appears to be another phase of the universal law of method in learning; it is a method of unifying the universal and the individual. What is its peculiarity?

An argument is the *indirect* unification of two of the foregoing attributes by means of the third. These attributes are *directly* unified with one another by means of judgment. A judgment is the decision of the mind in regard to the objective reality of a general idea. When it is said that the plant grows, that the object in the tree is a bird, a decision is made as to the objective reality of the general ideas, *grows* and *bird*. Such a decision argument is to justify. To argue is to present grounds for the mind's belief in the unity of the general and the individual. The ground of the mind's decision as to the unity of two ideas is their common relation to a third. The mark of reasoning is that there is conscious, indirect perception of unity.

If it is to be argued that the universal attribute, intense feeling, is found in the individual, Burns, a third idea intermediate between Burns and intense feeling — the particular — must be introduced. Let this particular be the class, poet. Intense feeling includes orators and others, as well as poets; and hence is universal in relation to poets. Poets contain the universal, intense feeling, and include Burns; hence the intense feeling must be in Burns. Thus the universal is in the individual through the particular. This kind of argument is called *Deduction*, a "leading down" from the universal through the particular to the individual.

If the universal, intense feeling is affirmed of all in the class poets, it must be by means of the individual Burns, and as many other poets as necessary to justify the inference. Burns, and each individual examined — all known to be poets — has united in him all the attributes common only to the class poets, and the universal, intense feeling, which is also common to the class poets but extends to other classes. These two elements being found in each individual examined, tends to establish the belief that all poets have intense feeling. This conclusion is the truth assumed in the preceding argument. The movement here is from the individual through the particular to the universal. This kind of argument is called *Induction*, "a leading into" a general conclusion from individuals.

Another movement is necessary to unify the particular and the individual — to prove that Burns was a poet. This is accomplished by means of the universal attribute — universal in relation to the individual. It must first be known that poets express, in artistic language, idealized feeling in imaginative forms. Next, these attributes must be sought for in Burns. These universal attributes identify Burns with the class poets. The movement of mind is that of discerning that the universal attributes of the individual are identical with the particular attributes of the class. Hence this kind of argument is called *Identification*.

Giving the foregoing arguments the formal statement of the Syllogism, they appear thus : —

Deduction :

> All poets have intense feeling ;
> Burns was a poet ;
> Therefore, Burns had intense feeling.

Induction :
> Burns was a poet;
> Burns had intense feeling;
> Therefore, all poets have intense feeling.

Identification :
> A poet expresses intense feeling through imaginative forms, in artistic language.
> Burns expressed intense feeling through imaginative forms, in artistic language.
> Therefore, Burns was a poet.

These three movements are not properly three arguments, but the triple cord of a single argument. Each is grounded in the truth established by the other two. Deduction has no force unless the first proposition is established by induction, and the second by identification. Induction has force only when its first proposition is established by identification, and the second by deduction. Identification has no meaning unless its first proposition is established by induction, and its second by deduction. The certainty of the conclusion in each separate movement in the argument depends, therefore, not only on the correctness of that movement, but on the correctness of those which have conditioned it. In the practical conduct of an argument, the three kinds of reasoning move together, supporting each other in the conclusion to be established. Fallacies usually arise from breaking this triple unity of the argument. An argument made by one of the processes may seem to be clinching when in fact it has no basis in premises well established by the other processes. Hence, the pupil, being trained to safe habits of argumentation must be challenged in both of the premises, as well as in the justness of the conclusion drawn from the premises.

The foregoing movements in the argument give rise to three methods of teaching by argumentation. While they move forward together, each should be distinct in consciousness to the teacher. These methods are so intimately related that it is questionable if they can be spoken of as distinct methods of teaching subjects; as, an inductive or a deductive method of teaching arithmetic, grammar, etc., for they are the intertwined movements through all subjects. The fact that the factor of two or more numbers is a factor of their sum may be proved by induction. The pupil should examine many cases, until he generalizes the facts into a law. Then, by deduction, the generalization made by induction must be shown to be necessarily true. By the examination of instances the pupil may infer by induction that all infinitives have a substantive use. This should also be established by deduction. And in these movements it will be necessary to settle the question as to whether a word in question is an infinitive. Note that in these examples deduction does not start from the truth generalized by induction, but from some universal above that, and descends to it as a particular. The universal of the induction is the particular of the deduction which clinches the induction. Thus the teacher in moving through any subject is constantly using all the methods.

It must not be supposed that argumentation is a method of thought to be used after the pupil has completed his discussion of the individual under description and narration, or after he has treated the general notion by the process of exposition. Argumentation is in and through all those processes. In fact it has been emphasized many times that all the processes discussed under the head of universal method are only phases of one movement. The three organic movements in the argument have, therefore, been implicit in all the foregoing discussions. This suggests further that the teacher need not wait till pupils study logic for an opportunity to train them to habits of correct reasoning. Logic may formulate the theory of reasoning, but it cannot supply the habit and structure of thought which should be formed in all studies.

These methods of teaching are so important as to justify a more detailed statement of —

THE PROCESSES IN AN ARGUMENT.

1. *Controlled by Relation of Extent.*

Deduction. — Proof in deduction is based on the axiom that whatever attribute is common to all the individuals of a class must be found in each individual of the class. It is impossible to believe that all statesmen are politicians and at the same time believe that this statesman is not a politician. To think that all horses are quadrupeds necessitates the thought that this horse is a quadruped. The conclusion is concerning the part of a whole; which part is affirmed, through the mediation of an idea more general than itself and less general than the whole, to have the same universal nature as the whole. To make this more distinct, picture the relations among the three ideas involved in this argument: Put all quadrupeds in a circle; then within this circle put another circle containing horses, and within the circle containing horses, select one horse. This one horse being in the circle of horses, which is in the circle of quadrupeds, must himself be in the circle of quadrupeds. He cannot be thought outside of the larger circle while he is thought in a circle within the larger one.

It thus seems that a deductive syllogism is absolutely conclusive. But it is not so unless (1) the premises are sound and (2) the unity of the two ideas is properly made in the third.

1. Because of its convincing force in itself, the student is too often satisfied without raising a question as to the foundation of the deduction in its premises. Deduction cannot increase the certainty of truth beyond the warrant of the induction and the identification on which it rests. At best it can only be said that what it affirms is true, provided something else is true. A speaker often makes a plausible argument because the unwary auditor does not stop to question the unwarranted assumption on which the argument rests. How many great questions have for years been settled on the current assumption that the Monroe Doctrine is final truth! Foreign immigration is restricted on the assumption that whatever is a burden to American institutions should be prohibited. This may be a sound major premise; but certainly it is not a final truth concerning the policy of a nation. It might be said

that a nation should do all it can in a hospitable and philanthropic way to advance the civilization of the world, forgetting its own selfishness in the larger movement. The assumption of this premise might lead to the same conclusion as the preceding; but it shows here that unquestioned premises are not always unquestionable. The campaign speaker on free trade or protection often slyly beguiles his hearer into the assumption of premises which are sure to clinch the argument on his side of the question. Do you want British free trade? Assumption: British free trade is a bad thing. Do you not want to buy where you can buy cheapest? Assumption: Free trade makes cheap buying.

Man's practical life is always regulated by the major premises which he assumes and to which he adheres. At this point the teacher's opportunity and responsibility are great. Not only should the pupil be trained to caution in the assumption of premises; but he should be brought to adopt the highest spiritual development as the major premise from which to argue all questions of individual, social, or political conduct. It is often urged, and with reason, that pupils should have instruction in civics preparatory to citizenship; but no better preparation can be given than that of training them to survey cautiously the premises of action in a given case. They thus become free from party bias, the political rabble, and the demagogue; and what is a more immediate and pressing necessity? A free citizen, to be free, must be able to ground his action in a universal truth which overshadows his immediate actions and his relations to his fellow-man. To this end careful training in assuming ultimate truth as a major premise in argument and action is indispensable ; as it is also indispensable in searching out truth for truth's sake — in bringing the learner into unity with the world about him.

2. With accepted premises there may be a fallacy in the connection of the minor and major terms through the middle. The law here is that *if the two terms are united in the middle, one may be affirmed of the other; if not so united, the affirmation cannot be made. If one is included in the middle and the other excluded, one may be affirmed not to be the other; but if both are excluded from the middle, no affirmation can be made.*

The pupils should be trained to picture the relation of the three terms, universal, particular, and individual ; or as they are named in the syllogism, the major, middle, and minor terms.

Suppose pupils are to prove that this object, a bird, is warm-blooded. The thought moves from this object to bird, and then to warm-blooded animals. But the movement is formally tested in the reverse order by means of the syllogism ; thus : —

>All birds are warm-blooded ;
>This object is a bird ;
>Therefore, it is warm-blooded.

Now require pupils to put in a circle all warm-blooded animals ; and within this circle another containing birds, as required by the first proposition. This circle is smaller than the first because many warm-blooded animals are not birds. Next put this bird in the smaller circle, as required by the last proposition. The mind cannot think this bird in the smaller circle, which is in the larger, and at the same time think this bird outside the larger.

Testing the following by the same means we find a different result : —

> All mammals are warm-blooded ;
> This bird is warm-blooded ;
> Therefore, this bird is a mammal.

Again imagining all warm-blooded animals in a circle ; and within this circle a smaller circle of mammals, as the first proposition requires. The circle of mammals is smaller and falls completely within the circle of warm-blooded animals, since there are many other animals besides mammals that are warm-blooded. The second proposition requires this bird to be placed in the circle of warm-blooded animals ; but whether it falls within or without the circle of mammals is not expressed by the proposition. Hence the conclusion cannot be drawn that this bird is a mammal, or that it is not. Simply no affirmation can be made.

So much will suggest the method of testing all possible cases that may arise under the deductive syllogism. Jevon's Science Primer of Logic will aid the teacher who is interested in making the most of this kind of drill. Again let it be said that the teacher must not wait till the formal study of logic to give training in this form of thought. Theory is not the thing most needed; it is training to a form of conception — to conceive with logical precision the unity of two ideas through a third. The opportunity is not only offered throughout the common school course, but it is a necessity of that course. Pupils can perform this feat of thought in simple cases from the very outset of the course.

Induction. — Proof through induction is based on the belief that what is essential to the part must be common to the whole. And this is based on our faith that the world is an organic, systematic whole. If this faith were removed, all induction would be impossible. To argue by induction is to make the strongest appeal to this faith.

A single act of deduction is conclusive; but a single act of induction may create only probability. What the single act lacks in convincing power must be made good by the repetition of inductive acts. This seems a clumsy and unsatisfactory process, but there comes a point in the accumulation of examples at which the feeling of probability becomes certainty. In fact, the mind has so much faith in the uniformity of nature that the feeling of certainty arises before it is warranted by the facts observed. One most important point in training pupils to correct habits of induction is that of checking hasty conclusions. This was illustrated in the lesson sketched on the plural of the word *boys*. Pupils might infer at once that all plurals were made by adding the letter *s*. Certainly they would do so after a few other such plurals were studied.

Their conclusion should be disturbed by the study of words forming their plurals in *es*. Next time they will be inclined to withhold judgment till more complete observation. Yet soon they will conclude that all plurals are formed by adding *s* or *es*. This conclusion will again be disturbed; and so with others till all plural forms are reached. Such is the opportunity constantly offered to train to caution in making conclusions by induction.

The number of individuals examined through which a conclusion is reached may range from one to all, except one. If all were examined, the process would be generalization and not induction. Induction is the leap of faith from the known to the unknown; it bridges the chasm between the realm of observation and what lies beyond observation. This illustrates again that reason is a phase of the mind's freedom in identifying itself with the world lying beyond. It can know the world and that kind of truth which lies beyond the range of observation and imagination.

There are two phases of induction: (1) that which concerns itself with the connection among attributes in objects, called *analogy*, and (2) that which concerns itself with the connection among objects themselves.

1. By analogy it is concluded that when a given number of attributes are connected in a given object, and part of the same number are found in another object, the others of the first object are inferred to be in the second. The conclusion in analogy is affirmed on the ground of (a) the

number of resembling attributes in two objects; and (b) the causal connection between the points of resemblance.

a. The greater the number of attributes found to correspond in the two objects the more confidently may those not observed in one of the objects be inferred to be present in that object. This is reasoning by mere resemblances. If it be known that a piece of chalk is light, white, brittle, and can be used to make a mark, on seeing a second object, or any number of them, which has the first three marks, the fourth will be inferred to be present. To argue, then, by analogy, in this the lowest phase, is to present as many points of resemblance between the known and the unknown terms as possible.

This phase of analogy, that of mere resemblance, is used much by people who have but little power of thought. No argument is more convincing to this class than an example, however superficial the resemblances. To give an example of a man who is profane, who tells falsehoods, and who belongs to a certain political party, is sufficient to convince the unthinking, who do not know the other adherents of the same faith, that they too are profane and untruthful.

b. The number of attributes, however, is not the safest basis of inference. Much more depends on the causal connection in the points of resemblance. If a strange animal were found to have a peculiar structure of the skeleton, it would be safer to infer that all of the class had the same structure, than to infer that the class had the same color as the specimen examined; even if they resembled in many other superficial points. Inference from analogy becomes more certain as the points of resemblance become more fundamental. If the objects under question can be shown to have a similarity to the known term of comparison in a single essential respect, it is more convincing than resemblance in many superficial attributes. Therefore, in arguing by analogy, the points of comparison must be shown to be essential to the nature of the object. When this cannot be done, the mere force of the number of points of resemblance must be resorted to. If it is to be proved, by its analogy to the earth, that Jupiter is inhabited, the accumulation of all the points of resemblance would have weight; but to show that Jupiter is like the earth in those points that condition human life, would be far more convincing.

2. The second phase of induction, that which connects objects rather than attributes of an object, has two phases corresponding to those in analogy; conclusions based on (a) number of objects resembling; and (b) on the causal connection between the objects.

a. The conclusion in this phase of induction is based on the mere force of accumulated examples. The first orange observed being yellow does not justify the assertion that all oranges are yellow. But by repeated observations, the mind confidently extends this attribute to all oranges; and does so without perceiving any necessary connection between the color and the orange. We believe only on the ground that if there had been oranges of other colors we should have chanced upon them. As the number increases, probability grows into certainty. Not that this can ever become the certainty of demonstration, for the opposite of what is affirmed may always be conceived; but the mind rests satisfied in its conclusion. As in the first phase of analogy the force of the argument is in the number of points of resemblance, so in this the convincing power is in the mere number of examples.

b. The highest phase of induction seeks a causal connection as the basis of inference. The more fundamental the relation of the attributes observed, the fewer examples are needed. It is sometimes impossible to discover an essential relation of the attribute under question to the object in which it is found; as, why an orange is yellow. In such cases there is no appeal from the mere force of numbers. But in most cases, arguing by induction consists in pointing out the essential relations of the property under discussion to the others in the examples produced. When the manner of the working of the cause is obvious, there is little difficulty in the process; as, in the rain wetting the ground. We see in the nature of rain why this effect is produced, and have no hesitancy in saying that rain will always produce this effect. The relation that the valves sustain to the function of the heart is easily determined, and that all hearts have such parts is readily inferred. But the manner of the working of causes cannot in all cases be detected; as, a tree growing more rapidly in one kind of soil than the same kind of tree has been observed to grow in another kind of soil. In such a case it must be shown that there exists a cause and effect relation. We may not see how they are connected, but to know that they are necessarily connected is safe ground for the induction.

When the manner of the working of a cause cannot be detected, it becomes difficult to decide that there is really a cause and effect relation. Especially is this true in complex phenomena; for in this the essential is entangled with the accidental. Logicians have given us four methods of detecting the presence of this relation.[1]

Identification.—This is the process of deciding whether an object is or is not one of a class. The purpose is not to form a class, but to find the class in the individual for the knowledge of the individual. A strange plant is found, and the first impulse of the mind is to class it. A course of reasoning follows for that purpose. A common illustration is found in a parsing lesson. Is this word an infinitive or a noun? is the type of question to be argued.

Proof by identification rests on the perception of the identity of essential attributes in the individual and the class. For instance, an infinitive expresses an abstract object and time; this word expresses an abstract object and time; therefore it is an infinitive. The proof is based on the axiom that things equal to the same thing are equal to each other. The first step in the process is to expound the class to which the individual is supposed to belong; the second step is to describe the individual; and the third is to ascertain by comparison whether the individual contains all the attributes essential to the class.

[1] See Mill's Logic, pp. 278-291.

The teacher has constant opportunity for drill in this form of reasoning. In the study of animals the pupil may class the bat with birds. He should be required to formulate the essential ideas constituting birds, and then test the bat as to these essential points. The likeness observed in superficial attributes must yield to the likeness among essential attributes. The mere fact of having wings is less essential to life than internal structure. A certain movement of water is classed as an ocean current; and the student must be required to justify his classification by showing identity of essential attributes. Why not class it as a river? a wave? An expression in the reading lesson is called a figure of thought; then require pupils to enumerate the essential ideas of a figure, and find those ideas in the expression under question; noting also those not essential and not common to the class figures. It is worth much to the teacher to be conscious of his mental movement, for then it may be directed and cultivated with precision and effect.

2. *Process controlled by Relation of Cause and Effect.*

Another view of argumentation has practical guidance for the teacher. The preceding phases of an argument, deduction, induction, and identification, grow out of the relation of the extent of the ideas involved — individual, particular, and universal. There is consciousness of a mediating idea. But all this rests on a deeper truth — the organic connection of things in themselves. The primary question is, What is there in the nature and relation of the things in themselves to constitute the unity sought? The real relations of objects in the world is the reason for connecting them in a proposition. The primary reason for the relation asserted is found not in the relation of whole and part, or the relative extent of ideas, as it seemed in the discussion of arguments on the preceding basis, but in the constituting elements of the objects and ideas themselves. All the relations of an object which bring it into connection with another — the interdependencies of things — are the basis for connecting them in a proposition. All such relations, dependencies, interactions, are comprehended under the relation of cause and effect. This is the underlying truth assumed in the discussions of the preceding processes. There the mental movement was emphasized; now the relations among things themselves which control that movement are to be set forth. The relations of individual, particular, and universal are not to be left out of sight; only the cause and effect relation among them to be emphasized.

Suppose on looking out in the morning we find the ground wet and wish to explain it. This can only be done by applying concepts. Let us try the concept rainfall. This concept has for its content the idea water falling in drops from the clouds, caused by a definite condition of the air, and producing a definite effect in falling. No general idea of rain can be formed without these constituent ideas. The particular fact observed seems to answer to the effect in the concept. If, on close inspection, it has all the marks of the effect in the concept,

the other elements must also be present in the concept
— water falling from clouds, and this caused by certain
conditions of the air. Hence we conclude that the particular phenomenon of last night had all the elements of
the general idea, and bore the relation of effect to all the
other constituent ideas. We, therefore, conclude that it
rained. This individual effect before us is thus connected,
through the particular, with its universal, by the relation
of cause and effect; the effect before us being the individual, the rainfall of last night the particular, and rainfall
in general the universal.

Changing the application of the concept, suppose that in
the afternoon the weather is warm, the air is moist, and
the clouds begin to form. We find in this what answers
to the cause in the concept. We have reason to affirm
that the other elements in the concept will be present. If
we observe the falling drops of water, we supply the two
elements, the cause and the effect of the falling. Note
here that the cause is not the same as in the other examples, the falling itself being a cause in the first, and an
effect in the second. In reasoning each element in the
concept bears in turn the relation of cause or effect, as one
or the other is the basis for seeking the unknown element.
The clouds and the falling drops may be either cause or
effect to the element sought.

In the above example the universal element was sought
through the particular to explain the individual — the
syllogistic movement under the relation of cause and
effect. The same relation of cause and effect is the basis

of connection when the individual is sought in the universal in order to establish the truth of the universal — the inductive movement under the relation of cause and effect. Suppose there is to be proved this universal proposition: "All tyrants are selfish men." This must be proved by individuals from the class tyrants. Caesar being a tyrant and selfish is in the line of proof. But how does this tend to establish the proposition? Not merely as an example; for then it were as well to argue that all tyrants are good generals, because Caesar was a tyrant and a good general. There must be shown in this example some causal connection between tyranny and selfishness; as, Caesar's selfishness, his desire to control others to his own good, necessarily manifested itself in the form of tyranny. More examples would strengthen the argument; but each example derives its force from the relation that selfishness as a cause bears to tyranny as an effect. Thus we are convinced that, in general, wherever we find the cause selfishness we will find its effect tyranny When we wish to prove that all plants are organic, we do so by showing in the concrete examples observed, that there is an essential, a causal relation existing between plant life and the organs through which that life manifests itself.

Thus, on this new basis of cause and effect there are two classes of arguments: those in which the cause is given to establish the effect; and those in which the effect is given to establish the cause. The first are called *A Priori* arguments, or arguments from Antecedent Probability; the second are called *A Posteriori* arguments, or arguments from Experience.

A Priori Arguments. — The *a priori* arguments are arguments from cause to effect, explaining either what has happened or what will likely happen. Thus we may prove that with the increase of popular education there will be a decrease in crime; education having in itself a nature, a force, a cause, such as to produce this as an effect. That a certain candidate will be elected may be predicted from his high character, or the principles which he embodies. That prosperous times are or are not produced by a change in governmental administration is to be proved by determining whether there is in the nature of the case a sufficient cause. Tourgee urges, in his "Appeal to Caesar," that there will arise future trouble with the South from the cause now present — the multiplication of the negro population. The guilt or innocence of an accused person in court may be largely established by the *a priori* argument. It is difficult to convict a person whose character is such as to furnish no antecedent probability for the crime alleged; while it is easy to do so where there is such a probability. If the man accused of murder is shown to have hated the murdered intensely, and would gain great riches by committing the crime, there would be a strong motive to the deed. This, however, would not prove his guilt, but would show only why he may have committed the murder. To give such evidence its greatest force, it must be shown that there is nothing in the accused person's character to oppose the free action of the motive; as, fear of the law, or high moral character.

Law of inference from cause. — Whenever there is a known cause its full effect must be inferred, provided there are no hinderances. When there are hinderances, the effect is decreased in proportion to the hinderance, to the point of prevention. The degree of probability depends on the strength of the cause after the hinderance is overcome. To prove the absence of cause, or that the cause is neutralized by opposing forces, is to destroy all probability whatever. If a man has no motive to theft, or is confined so that the act would be impossible, he could not be charged with such a crime.

Physical causes are more certain to be followed by their effects than moral causes. The warmth of the sun and the moisture in spring will clothe the earth in verdure; but whether a nation at enmity against another will bring war is not so certain. In the realm of volition, so many and so complex are the motives, and so many of them hidden from view to all except the person choosing, that the connection of cause and effect is very uncertain. If all motives could be taken into account, the resulting effect in action could be as certainly inferred as the effect of a cause in the physical world. The uncertainty of prevision in history arises from this cause. The forces are so diffused and complex that their resultant is difficult to estimate. Besides so many latent forces in human character must be left out altogether.

A common fallacy in argumentation under the law of

inference from cause is the assumption that one of two or more effects which may seem to have equal connection with the cause is the effect which is to follow. Which of these effects will follow is the very point in question. Or, of two or more causes which may equally well account for the effect, one is assumed as the cause. Which of these is the real cause is to be proved by the argument. This fallacy is called, "begging the question." One writer may urge the system of land holding as the cause of the discontent of the country, while another finds the cause in foreign immigration ; and a third is sure that railroad monopolies are responsible. Each assumes one cause, and finding that it tends in the desired direction, expects his readers to infer it to be the sole cause ; while other causes may be shown to bear with equal force, and all of them, or some cause fundamental enough to include all the minor causes, might be a better basis for inference than any one presented. Another form of this fallacy is the assumption that one circumstance is the cause of another when it is only a concomitant. Statistics are presented to prove that illiteracy is the cause of crime ; while both illiteracy and crime may be common effects of the low character of the persons enumerated in the statistics. People do not read; it is observed that they have no libraries ; and the second fact is thought to explain the first, while the absence of the reading and the library may be concomitant facts of a common cause; as, the pressure of hard manual labor ; the desire for sensual indulgence ; sluggish state of mind.

A fruitful source of such fallacies as the above is the desire or prejudice of the one who makes the argument. To a greater extent than one is conscious, will he select from probable causes the one which he desires to be the cause. The heart has arguments that the head knows not of. A bad motive is generally assumed to explain the action of those to whom we are opposed; and good motives to explain the actions of those with whom we agree. No candidate for office expects just inferences from the opposite party. Even the philanthropist, in carrying on some benevolent enterprise, is gratuitously supplied with selfish motives. When many good reasons will readily account for an action, the mind is too often determined in its choice, not by the careful estimate of the relation of cause and effect, but by the wish that a certain motive be the cause. The President may favor or veto a certain measure, and his course be explainable either by a desire for the general good or for some selfish gain. Party affiliations will cause one party to praise him for his disinterested loyalty and justice; while with the other, party prejudice finds, in the position taken, nothing but selfishness or cowardice. When either the advantages of Free Trade or of Protective Tariff are to be proved against the other, many beneficial effects are assumed that could as easily be explained by other conditions; and which would be so explained if the case had not been prejudiced — prejudged — by the desires. The caution needed here is that in estimating an argument the prejudices of the writer or speaker be taken into account; and that in making the argument those assumptions which prejudice intrudes be excluded. The remedy for this fallacy is to love truth more and victory less. The man who wishes to be really, not apparently, successful in debate must come to the question with an earnest desire to find the real relation of cause and effect involved solely for the sake of the truth. A debating club in which a question is discussed for the sake of victory is not conducive to that attitude of mind necessary to effective argument. The hypocrisy of the judgment in its pretense of reasons blinds it to the real relations and reasons when engaged in an actual contest for truth. Much of the so-called drill in debating is only a drill in fluency of words and manipulation of fallacies.

The teacher's responsibility and opportunity through *a priori* argument are revealed by the foregoing. The teacher must not wait for the theory of argumentation before rigid drill in this process of thought is given; nor turn aside from the daily work for an opportunity. It occurs as a daily necessity in almost every lesson; and the teacher need only to be conscious of the movement to give the mind the correct habit and power of *a priori* thinking. In studying the Gulf Stream, its universal attributes must be sought; say, its effect on the civilization of Europe. One means of ascertaining this is the *a priori* method of thought; what would necessarily be expected from the nature of the Gulf Stream? The World's Fair had universal elements in it; effects that reach the nations of the earth. The problem is to find from the nature of the thing itself what this effect is to be. When a century has passed and the fruit has been borne the other method of thought may be turned back upon it. These are types of questions and thought movements that occur almost constantly in every subject and in every phase of school work.

A Posteriori Arguments.— These are arguments from effect to cause, explaining why something is, or why something has happened. The effect is known, and the cause which produced it is sought. The *a posteriori* and the *a priori* arguments each presents the subject-matter under the relation of cause and effect. In the *a priori*, known causes point to unknown future events, or to some known effect which the known cause explains; while in the *a posteriori* argument the effect is known and the cause sought.

Whether in the physical or in the spiritual world, everything is thought as caused. We have seen that cause and effect are correlative terms; that both are essential elements in every concept, so that when one is present, the mind naturally tends to connect the other. A failure in the wheat crop, a decrease in the price of merchandise, Chinese immigration, the movement of the locomotive engine, the engine itself, Gladstone's attitude toward home rule — all force the mind to seek the explanation in their respective causes.

Inference of cause from effect is based on the different thought relations involved in thinking. The whole may be inferred from the part, or the part from the whole; the substance from the attribute, or the attribute from the substance; from likenesses other likenesses, or from differences other differences; from an effect its adequate cause; from adaptation may be inferred purpose. From the presence of the whole of a steam engine, certain parts may be safely inferred; or with a part of it present, the whole will be suggested. The attribute yellow being present in a distant field, some substance, as wheat or clay, will be suggested; and the substance, wheat-field, will suggest some accompanying attribute. Likeness in color, form, texture, and parts of two kinds of fruit will suggest likeness as to flavor and odor; and differences in the first respects named will suggest differences in the second. From the moving train, the steam as an adequate cause of the motion is inferred. From the adaptation of an anchor to grapple in the bed of the ocean the inference is readily made that some one designed it.

But in all these cases the inference is based on the relation of cause and effect. The adaptation in the anchor is caused by its purpose; that in the nature of the fruits which causes them to be alike in certain respects will cause them to be alike in other respects; that which usually conditions or causes the presence of the yellow color under the conditions observed is still the cause; and whatever there is in the nature of the engine to necessitate the relation of whole and part is permanent in causing that relation.

Laws of inference from effect. — The degree of force in the *a posteriori* argument varies with the certainty of the causal relation on which the inference is based. This depends on (1) the number and complexity of the causes which may produce the effect; and (2) the efficiency and reality of the cause.

1. A cause may be inferred from an effect with certainty when the effect is such that only one cause will produce it. We may argue conclusively that the oak is produced from an acorn; that steam is caused by heat; that the burned house has been on fire; there being no other cause for each phenomenon. The train is moving, and steam may be inferred as the cause; but not conclusively, for there are other forces that may be moving it; as, men, horses, electricity, gravity; but when there are many causes, either of which or a combination of which may produce the effect, the inference becomes less certain as the number and complexity increase. As a rule, the number and complexity of causes increase in passing from the physical to the spiritual world. Especially is it difficult to assign causes for social phenomena, so manifold and subtile are the moving forces. And nowhere are fallacies more common. They arise either from a lack of a comprehensive grasp of complex causal relations; from a prejudice which leads to the assumption of one cause in preference to another; or from the assumption of one cause instead of a group acting together.

2. In the argument from resemblance, a cause may be inferred with certainty when the resemblances are essential. On the ground that Caesar was selfish and a tyrant, it might safely be inferred that another ruler who was

selfish was also a tyrant, there being a causal relation between selfishness and tyranny. Glass is transparent and brittle ; but it does not follow that because water is transparent it is also brittle ; there being no essential relation between transparency and brittleness. In such cases the burden of proof consists in showing that the points of resemblance are so related to the nature of the object that they are constant marks of it. This may be done by establishing directly a causal relation, as in the case of selfishness and tyranny ; or by an accumulation of examples till the uniformity establishes a belief in a constant cause, as explained under Induction.

Attributes and objects are so often accidental accompaniments of each other without causal relation that arguments from example are fruitful sources of fallacies. The immature and the untrained mind, in their tendency to hasty conclusions, generally infer a causal relation where there is only an accidental coexistence ; as, —

Some intemperate man lives to a great age ; therefore, intemperance is conducive to longevity.

It rained on Monday and the two succeeding days of the week ; therefore, when it rains on Monday it will rain three days in the week.

A great man smokes ; therefore, smoking is manly.

Byron was licentious and a great poet ; therefore, licentiousness is favorable to poetic inspiration.

A man who believes the doctrines of a certain church is immoral ; hence, the doctrines of that church tend to produce immorality.

This kind of argument is much used by the sophist. The demagogue finds it an effectual means of carrying conviction to the minds of unthinking people. By means of it, he accounts for the dull or for the flourishing condition of the times ; the high or low prices of crops and merchandise ; the scarcity or the abundance of productions; the demand for labor or the difficulty with which it is obtained ; and gives the credit or the blame, as suits his purpose, to the party in power ; when the coexistence of the facts may be purely accidental. To prove the value of a classical over a scientific education, or *vice versa,* some eminent scholar is instanced who has pursued one of the courses ; while his eminence may be accounted for by a large number of causes ; as, natural endowment, more thorough discipline on account of superior teachers, social opportunities, combined effect of various studies, etc. The proof would be absolutely convincing if the same person could be the subject of each course ; for then the conditions would be identical ; or, if many examples under similar conditions from each course could be furnished. Through every phase of life, reasoning by example is a fruitful source of error in the lower order of thinkers, and hence an effective means of deception in the hands of the unprincipled.

Let the teacher note his opportunity and responsibility under this process as under the preceding. In teaching, when the case permits, the two processes move hand in hand. Both methods are necessary to make a complete argument. In the preceding example of the Gulf Stream, the effects on English civilization should be forecast from the nature of Gulf Stream by the *a priori* method; and this should be supported by noting facts in that civilization which point back to the Gulf Stream as cause. In history the question will arise, What was the effect of slavery on the industrial and social life of the people? This must be viewed in two relations: first, the effect to be expected from the nature of slavery; second, certain known present conditions which point back to slavery as the cause. It requires both movements to make the argument strong and complete. Pupils should be trained to support the argument from both sides. Only the *a priori* method can be used when the effects lie in the future; but in all other cases the two methods must support each other.

Finally, let it be observed that the movement of thought by the two preceding methods is only another phase of the universal law of method, in which the mind moves from the individual out to the universal, and back with the universal to the individual. These relations of cause and effect connect the individual with the universe about it.

THE PROCESS AS A COMPLEX WHOLE.

So far, under the head of method, we have considered the full round of the mind's activity on a given portion of subject-matter. There is a larger sense in which method is the movement of thought through the period of school life — the complex whole of the teaching process. This larger movement of thought must be in the mind of the teacher as a condition for knowing what the movement in detail must be. The larger movement is by steps, or stages of growth, along lines of thought running through school life. It is doubly complex, in that it has both coexisting and successive parts. This movement formulated is called the Course of Instruction, or the Course of Study; the word *course* suggesting the time element as the prominent factor.

The universal law of method controls here as it does in the "Specific Phases of the Process." The relation of unity between the pupil and the subject to be learned controls the teaching process in a given act of instruction; so the process as the complex whole of school life is controlled by the relations of unity between the *subject-matter* taken as a whole, and the *learner's* life considered in its entire compass. The subject-matter is the basis of the course; the growing pupil, the modifying factor. The first gives the lines which thread the course through from beginning to end; the second gives the stages of forward movement on those lines. The first is the warp, the second, the woof of the course. Objective existence, or subject-matter, determines the one; the subjective order of the pupil's unfolding determines the other.

THE OBJECTIVE FACTOR.

The subject-matter furnishing the material for the course is all objective existence, including mind as its own object. All existence stands over against the mind, and is the means for its discipline and its illumination. Hence, by an analysis of the field of existence, as the mind knows it, the subjects of instruction are to be organized; and the main lines of thought through the course to be determined.

Existence is first made knowable by being formed into bodies through the forces of cohesion and gravitation. Thus we know bodies as mere bodies extending in space. Following closely upon this is knowledge of bodies as to number. This is based on the repetition of the perception of objects — based on time as the preceding is based on space. Every object that is known must be known as existing in space and time. Viewing bodies as to their form and number gives rise to the line of *mathematics* in the course. The peculiarity of this study is that the attributes are universal, belonging to all objects in the universe; and are abstracted entirely from material bodies.

The mind next knows these bodies as acted on by physical forces — atomic force, molecular force, and gravitation. Viewing bodies thus gives rise to the line of *physical* science in the course. These attributes are universal as before, but cannot be abstracted from the material body.

While all bodies are acted on by physical force, some

are acted on by life force, producing living or organized bodies. Viewing bodies under the influence of this force gives rise to the line of *biological* science in the course. This science differs from the two preceding in that the ideas are not universal. This gives rise to the division into organized and unorganized beings. Living objects are still acted on by physical forces, and exist under mathematical relations. Hence all living bodies are treated in the lines of physical and mathematical studies.

Some of these living, organized beings are acted upon by spiritual or mind force, giving rise to *psychological* science, using the term in its broadest sense. The ideas here apply to still fewer objects. Such objects are still acted upon by life force and physical force, and exist under mathematical relations; and hence are subjects of discussion in all the preceding lines.

The world is a hierarchy of forces. Each is based in, and arises out of the preceding; and all may manifest themselves in the same object. These forces condition the order of knowing the object. An object cannot be known as to its nature and physical forces till it is first thought in space and time. Hence the physical sciences are based on mathematical sciences.

No organized or living being could exist as such, if it were not acted on by all the lower forces. A plant, to live, must be acted on by cohesion and chemical affinity. So that every living being must be known under the lower forces, and also under the mathematical relations, to be known at all. Hence the biological sciences are based upon the physical sciences, and through them on the mathematical sciences.

Every being acted on by mind force could not exist as such if not acted on by all the lower forces, vital and physical, and if not existing under mathematical relations. Hence to know a spiritual being implies a knowledge of it as a living being, a physical being, and a mathematical being.

All existence is organized under these relations and forces; and this determines the lines along which the pupil's thought must move in gaining a knowledge of the objective world. These lines are separated because a new force is operative in passing upward from matter to mind; they are unified in the fact that each lower relation and force is effective in all the succeeding. Man forms a distinct line because spiritual force is manifested; but he is connected with all lines, since he is not only treated as a spiritual being, but as a biological being, as a physical being, and as a mathematical being. Plants and animals form a distinct line because of the presence of a force not found below them, and the absence of a force found above them. They are treated not only as biological beings, but as physical and mathematical beings. Thus arise the lines of study and the unity among them, giving the following course of study: —

Subjects.
1. Mathematical Science — Time and Space — the Field of Creation.
2. Physical Science — Matter and Physical Force.
3. Biological Science — Matter — Physical Force and Life Force.
4. Psychological Science — Mind Force.

By the same process as the foregoing, each of these lines may be divided until the detail of studies is reached, which is usually given in the school curriculum. There is a force which divides physical science into physics and chemistry; one that divides biological science into botany, zoölogy, and human physiology, etc. Space forbids such detail here. Summing up at once the result that would be reached, to the extent of the public school course, it stands about as follows: —

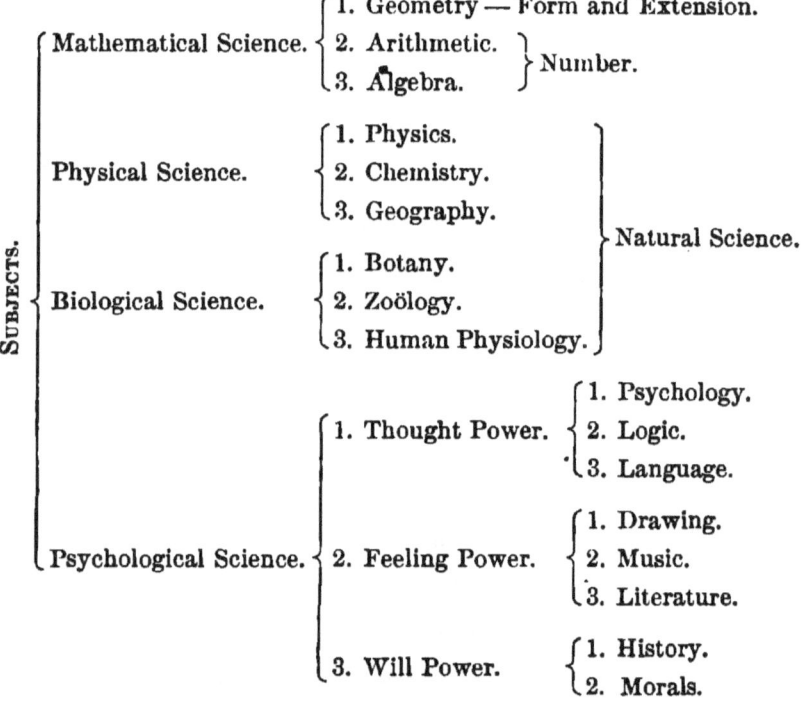

Before the course of study is complete, each of these branches must be traced out into its logical relation of parts until parts are reached sufficiently narrow for a single lesson. For instance, language studies are divided into three classes, accordingly as the language form is viewed in relation to an idea or in relation to a thought, or whether the form and thought taken in their unity, are viewed in relation to the effect which the speaker desires to produce. This gives rise to word study, sentence study, and discourse study. These again divide; as, in discourse study there is the science and the art — the science treated in rhetoric; and the art, the science applied, in reading and composition; the first being the interpretation of discourse, and the second the construction. Continuing this process of logical division, subject-matter will be reached that can be compassed in the plan of a single recitation. When all subjects are thus reduced the basis of the course of study is formed.

Such a plan of dividing and unifying the whole field of knowledge makes the course organic and systematic; giving it completeness and symmetry. Thus it is freed from bias, caprice, and custom.

The Subjective Factor.

From the foregoing it appears that the student should begin his work with mathematical studies; completing these, he should next take the lowest physical science; and thus move through the subjects in the order of conditioning and conditioned, completing each before beginning the next. While such is the logical order, it is not the learner's order; chiefly because of his unfolding power of thought. This factor is so effective that, instead of pursuing each line through which logically conditions the next, all the lines are carried abreast. The child on entering school takes a cross section of all the lines,—that phase of each of them which is adapted to the faculties then most active, and to the knowledge then possessed. He can advance but a little way in each before he falters from deficiency of knowledge or power of thought. Then he is compelled to turn back to pursue as far as possible another line. These forward movements are so insignificantly short as compared to his movements from one line to another that his course of study is crosswise of the logical course. When more power has been gained each separate logical line is pursued relatively longer. This movement forward on lines begins, after awhile, to overshadow the movement from one line to another. Finally, in university work, he specializes — feels his way along one line of thought out towards its limit.

At the outset of the pupil's course, the field seems to be broader, since the pupil is compelled to range over the whole extent of knowledge; but the content is shallow. In the last part of his course the field seems narrow, being limited to a single line; but the content is deep. And since the content is deep, the field, while seeming narrow, is the whole extent of existence. The universal attributes in the line studied root themselves out into all being. So that while the special student expects to narrow his field, he has at the same time widened it by giving a universal meaning to the object studied. The university student seeks for universal content in the object, and this is universal in extent; while the primary pupil glides over universal extent, reaching only superficial content.

It is all a question of the unfolding order of the subject as determined by the developing mind. Or, what is the same thing, it is the degree of generality of the subject-matter as determined by the phase of the mind addressed. The broad phases of mental development — perception, understanding, and reason, dealing with, respectively, individuals, generals, and universals — give rise to the three phases of culture in the school system — common school, high school, and the university, treating respectively of common knowledge, science, and philosophy. This classification of schools is not intended to fit into that now existing, but is ideally based on the laws of thought. The classification does, however, fit fairly well the existing state of things. It would remove the line between the high school and our so-called universities upward, and thus elevate both.

These phases are broadly marked; but they are valid, being grounded in the phases of the mind's development from infancy to maturity; or, in the nature of knowledge as it presents itself in the three phases of the individual, the general, and the universal. For example, the child learns an individual cow, and soon others; and as he proceeds in learning individuals, makes them into small classes. At the same time, it learns a particular horse, and then others; and as before, makes them into a small class. And so with other objects; classifying in respect to superficial and obtrusive attributes. But all the time the individual classified is prominent in the child's consciousness. It is not consciously forming classes — seeking the general. Soon, these small classes are brought together into larger ones; increasing the extent of the class by dropping the superficial attributes of the content. The attributes become more general, and more fundamental. His thinking, we say, rises in generality. Soon his increasing group of animals grows into larger classes; and because the common attributes become more general, less obvious, and, therefore, the more to be searched for, his effort to classify becomes conscious; and he then begins to think scientifically — to form his science of animals — to study zoölogy. Thus, and at the same time, he builds up his knowledge of plants into the science of botany. Later, he unites the concept plant and the concept animal into that of living, organic being — dropping the uncommon, and therefore the most superficial attributes remaining; yet holding to the one most fundamental and most general. He is now a biologist. In these latter phases, he is passing through and out of the high school. Soon, he studies the laws of life in general. Spiritual laws are subsumed under laws of life; and we have a student reaching well up into the universal — a university student. This is an orderly unfolding without breaks; the divisions, as in all other cases, are made only for the convenience of thought.

Hence the movement of the mind from the individual to the universal is not only the law of movement in learning irrespective of the time required, but it is the law of growth in knowledge through the unfolding years of life. It may properly be said then that a course of study is the subject-matter arranged in the necessary order of the learner's movement from the period of childhood, when he grasps individuals as such through sense perception, to the time when he grasps, through reason, universals in individuals.

From this it appears that there are no higher subjects; only higher phases of the same subject. The study of form, treated in geometry, has its perceptive, imaginative, and experimental phase, suitable to the lowest grade of thinking. From this phase the subject, as it grows in the mind of the learner, increases in generality and depth of content until the highest mind may engage its best powers upon it. Geography has its perceptive and imaginative phase suitable to the child. In this phase he has an experience with individual objects within the range of sense-perception, and pictures the earth and the objects on it which lie beyond perception. Then follows a low phase of organizing and grouping into small unities, under superficial laws by simple judgment, the objects supplied by the preceding processes; at the same time enriching the work of sense-perception and the imagination. Thus continuing by degrees until the unity of the world is reached in a single principle. Instead of a multitude of things as at the beginning, the student at the end finds but one thing — the earth, inclusive of all other things studied in that line. This view of the earth in its organic unity, which includes its unity with the universe, requires the highest powers of the most gifted mind; and is a fit subject for the university; as the lowest phase mentioned is a fit subject for the primary grade. History has its picture and story side suitable for the child; and also its philosophic side suitable for a Hegel.

In a course of study, therefore, all lines of thought should begin at the beginning of the course. The lower phase of all subjects should be mastered while the student is in the lower phase of thought. For instance, the imaginative and constructive phase of geometry, called form work, should be as fully done as possible before the power of demonstration is developed. The perceptive and memory phase of Latin can be most economically completed while the pupil is in that phase; leaving the higher powers free for exercise on the higher phase of the subject.

An objection is often urged against pursuing all lines of work at the same time—form, drawing, number, plants, animals, etc., on the ground of the burden thus placed upon the child; and that it is better to be thorough in a few things than to be smatterers in many.

It is not for the teacher to say what the field of thought shall be. If ideas of form and number, and physical and vital forces, etc., are organically related in the world to be known, then it is not for the teacher to vote them in or out. Ideas of form run through all the other subjects; and if those ideas are not systematically taken care of in a line of their own they must be taught incidentally, and with interruption, as they occur in the other lines. The idea **triangle** is essential to plant work, animal work, geography, physiology, reading, psychology, etc.; hence the teacher must be delayed if the idea has not been disposed of in the systematic way. To gain an idea of the heart, and countless other things, the pupil must have the concept cone; and it is economy to supply him with this form of thought in a systematic way, lest he become a smatterer. Geography involves ideas of plants and animals which can be much more effectively treated in their own lines. A study of mind so much facilitates the reading and literature work as to justify systematic lessons on that subject. All this means that the course cannot be lightened by shirking it. These things are in the course, and while they may be refused statement and treatment in separate lines, they cannot be voted out, however burdensome the course may seem. It is only a question whether they receive systematic and effective treatment or haphazard and wasteful attention as they are stumbled onto in the progress of work. Whatever *is* in the course must be in the course.

It is misplaced sympathy to restrict the number of studies to make the work easy. It is more burdensome to confine the attention to one line than to give the change and variety of six lines. There is a false notion, too, that by confining the child to a few lines, considered most essential, as, reading, writing, and arithmetic, he will move proportionately more rapidly if the lines are decreased. This cannot be done for two reasons : first, the more rapid movement is naturally checked by the difficulty of the subject increasing more rapidly than the child's power of thought increases. All the lines can be carried as rapidly as his developing power permits the child to advance on any one line. Second, as indicated above, the lines omitted from the narrowed course are essential to the free movement in the lines selected. Even music, which seems to be slightly connected with the other branches, from the rest and bouyancy it gives to the mind, may be carried along without retarding the progress in other lines. So that all the studies that would be omitted under the false notion of economizing the child's strength may be gained without loss of time, while supporting the lines so much desired.

To be thorough in a few lines rather than a smatterer in many is a most deceptive argument. It thrusts in the face two horns of a dilemma, and in self-defense one of them is seized rather than to choose the other, forgetting that there may be a third choice. There is no such thing as being thorough in a few things without the knowledge of many. Besides, a student may be a smatterer in one line as easily as in two. To smatter is to study things as isolated; to be thorough is to run a principle through them. A student may smatter in the study of botany; he may study all things in their unity and thus not smatter. Herbert Spencer is a student of all lines, without smattering. Bacon said: "I have taken all knowledge to my province." The question is not the number of things to which the student gives his attention, but whether he unifies his subject-matter; and this means that he generalizes it. Specializing is not the end, but a means of universalizing. We do not specialize, because the whole field of knowledge is too broad to be compassed by one mind. The part seems to outrun man's powers as readily as the whole. A knowledge of the part requires a knowledge of the whole. Any part of knowledge is infinite in its relations. To know that particular tree requires a knowledge of mathematics, physics, chemistry, and biology; and these require a knowledge of languages. Also, there is required a knowledge of spiritual laws, whose analogies throw light on the tree life, and which forms the basis of knowledge and certainty of that which is thought to be found in the tree.

> "Flower in the crannied wall,
> I pluck you out of the crannies;—
> Hold you here, root and all, in my hand,
> Little flower — but if I could understand
> What you are, root and all, and all in all,
> I should know what God and man is."

A student cannot take up his specialty and treat it as isolated. The moment he reaches deep down, he finds universal truth; and this forces him to reach beyond his specialty for light. The student decides to be a chemist; and at once needs to be a good mathematician, physicist, biologist, linguist, and philosopher. We may hitch ahead a little our end of truth, but it is so connected with the other end that, one quadrant reached, and we shall go round in a circle unless we bring up the other end. Yet we are compelled to search for universal truth in the form of the particular. Therefore, these two seemingly antagonistic phases of the university idea — that the university views its subject-matter from the standpoint of the universal, and that it is a school of specialties — are organically interdependent. Universal truth must be arrived at by a process of division of labor. Each must locate his point in the sphere of knowledge and point out the curvature.

Thus the course of study is formed between the two poles of universal extent and universal content. The primary pupil views the world in its universal extent by means of superficial and limited content; the university student views the world in its universal content as found in limited extent. The child not being able to reach a single unifying principle, not even anything less than a multiplicity of unifying principles, must leave its objects isolated, or in a multiplicity of groups. Even in the latter case it is unconscious unification; so that practically the world is a world of individuals. The university student seeks in limited extent a single principle which is the unity of the whole; and thus grasps the universe in each object and is relieved from the necessity of seizing it in detail.

It thus appears, as we should expect, that the universal law of method controls, not only the concrete act of teaching, but the whole course of instruction. The course of instruction is nothing but the universal law written large. This law, therefore, ought to solve the many problems arising in relation to the school curriculum, as the following: —

The problem of concentration. — The theory of "concentration," from which so much is now promised, as usually taught and practiced, is but the wavering image of the universal law of method. True concentration is not the strained and mechanical bringing together of diverse subject-matter into the same recitation, but fixing the attention on all the relations of the given subject, and thus drawing into the movement the other subjects required for the mastery of the one under consideration. In the true unifying process, emphasis must be given to the content and not to the extent of subject-matter; whereas, superficial concentration emphasizes the diversity of matter which may be disposed of during a given period. In teaching a plant, the teacher must not say to himself, "Now I must bring into the discussion geometry, literature, theology, etc."; but rather, "Now I must press the pupil's attention close to the relations which constitute the plant." If this should involve the facts and laws of geometric forms, let it be so; if this should reveal the infinite life, appealing as a poem to the sense of the beautiful, it must be well; if this should manifest infinite wisdom and supernatural power, theology has found its way into the movement without awkward circumlocution to make a place for it. If the thing be taught in the only way it can truly be taught, whatever subjects are needed will inevitably be drawn into the process.

The problem of enriching the course of study. — Enriching the elementary course of instruction, recently discussed so much, especially by the Committee of Ten, is only a question of obedience to the universal law of learning. As already illustrated in the discussion of the law, it would bring the elements of the so-called higher branches, such as geometry, general history, literature, botany and astronomy, into the very beginning of the course; while it would postpone, and thereby give place to the preceding, the more abstruse phases of the so-called lower subjects. There is a phase of astronomy more elementary — in terms of the law less general — than a phase of arithmetic; and it would enrich the course to have astronomy brought down in the place of that phase of arithmetic which can make no appeal to the pupil because too abstract and general for his concrete way of thinking. What the soul of the pupil needs for sustenance at a given time must be administered unto it, irrespective of tradition or of the logical symmetry of the subject. The course of study is too often considered as an objective arrangement of real things; whereas it is but the successive transformations throughout which the pupil passes in his progress towards self-realization. No external fixed something must be set over against the pupil's pulsating and plastic life. To have in the course of study eight years of arithmetic, two of algebra, and one of geometry; and four years of grammar, two of rhetoric, and one of literature may satisfy the lover of objective system, but such is forbidden by the subjective course in the pupil's development. The law of the pupil's learning demands that he have geometry, literature and science on his entrance into school. By nature's method he has made a respectable beginning in these before entering school; and no valid argument can be made for stopping his education simply because he is sent to school.

The nine conferences of experts, organized by the Committee of Ten to report on the first twelve years of the course of instruction, unanimously expressed a "desire to have the elements of their subjects taught earlier than they now are." For instance, "The Conference on Physics, Chemistry, and Astronomy urge that nature studies should constitute an important part of the elementary school course from the very beginning." And other Conferences report in the same spirit.

This unanimity is reached by university men and specialists in the subjects on which the report is made; and hence it is made from interest in the subject. The kindergartner, at the other extreme of the course, whose specialty is the child's development, had reached the same conclusion long before there was a Committee of Ten. The best elementary schools have been doing, under the pressure of the child's collective interests, just what those who occupy higher eminence in the subjects of study are now recommending. Hence, what is called enriching the course of study is only one of the many phases of the true law under discussion thrown to the surface where it may be easily discerned.

The problem of the correlation of studies. — Correlation of studies has reference to the organic relation of lines of thought running through the course, while enriching the course has reference to the unfolding of single lines of thought. This can have no other explanation than that given under the universal law of learning, and it will be found amply illustrated in the discussion of the law. The living world is made up of interrelated facts and forces, and, in bringing the pupil into unity with that world, his mental relations must correspond to the world which he thinks. And if the pupil press each topic, which he is considering, continuously out into its universal relations, he will necessarily fuse together all lines of investigation. We need not trouble ourselves about correlating studies; they will correlate themselves when they are truly taught. If the geography of the Southern states be pressed out into its wealth of relations — pressing the universal into the individual — it will necessarily cross over into the Civil War; and if the history of the Civil War be properly considered, the geography of the Southern states must furnish some of the essential relations. And if at this stage of history study the geography work has not prepared the way for the needed relation; or if at this stage of geography study the history work has not prepared the way for the needed geographical relation, the two subjects are not properly correlated. The needed relations in pushing a subject out towards its universal meaning determine what subjects must be pursued parallel, and what phases of each subject are needed at a given stage of advancement in any other subject. Correlation, then, is putting such subjects side by side at a given time in the course as will help to bring to view the universal relations involved in the study of any one of them. What these mutually helpful studies are, and what phases must come together in time, can be ascertained only by noting the ever-widening relations of each subject studied, and estimating the extent to which it penetrates every other.

The problem of educational values. — This topic assumes that subjects have different educational values, either in kind or degree, or both. At one time it was supposed that Greek, Latin, and mathematics had the highest and equal worth among subjects. Scientists have recently made a healthful protest, claiming for their subject equal educative power; and along with this, history and literature have been admitted to equal rank with the others. And then came the generalization that all subjects have equal educational value; that the chief matter is the method of study; that one is as disciplinary and enlightening as the other, if taught as thoroughly and in the same spirit. President Baker, speaking with reference to the report of the Committee of Ten, of which he was a member, says : "I cannot endorse expressions that appear to sanction that the choice of subjects in secondary schools may be a matter of comparative indifference. . . . All such statements are based upon the theory that, for the purposes óf general education, one study is as good as another, — a theory which appears to me to ignore Philosophy, Psychology and Science of Education. It is a theory which makes education formal, and does not consider the nature and value of the content. . . . The relation between the subjective power and the objective — or subjective — knowledge is inseparable and vital. On any other theory for general education, we might well consider the study of Egyptian hieroglyphics as valuable as that of physics, and Choctaw as important as Latin." He further adds that, "If rightly understood, the majority of the committee rejected the theory of equivalence of studies for general education."

The assumption of equivalence may hold for practical purposes among the few great trunk lines of thought. Who cares to debate the relative value of mathematics and science, science and language, or language and history! The difficulty arises when we descend into details of subordinate subjects and phases of subjects. In the details of school work, what to select and with what prominence to treat the point when selected, are most trying difficulties. The difficulty increases as the square of the distance from the organic centers of the world's thought to the trivial matter selected for a given recitation.

All this is a question of educational values, and must be determined by the law of bringing the pupil into unity with the world about him. A subject has value in proportion to its universality. Washington's fit of anger towards his officer has little value when compared to his Farewell Address, because it lacks universal content. The study of French has more value than the study of Canadian French, because wider relations appear to the pupil and a freer outlook disclosed. To decide between the value of the study of mathematics and natural science requires a decision as to their universality and the largeness of life possible to the student through each of the studies. Whether a student devote his life to the study of the ganglionic centers of a leech or to the ganglionic centers of

Greek life — its politics, philosophy, and literature — is a question as to which reveals to him most fully his own higher destiny. Since the pupil is to find his true self in the thought and spirit of the world about him, whatever subject reflects in his consciousness the widest realm of that thought and spirit must have for him the greatest value.

The problem of morals in the public school. — There has always been a feeling that moral instruction belongs to the school course; but how to organize it in with other subjects has given the teacher no little concern. This difficulty arises from overlooking the fact that all good teaching is essentially ethical, together with the erroneous conception that man's moral nature is only one side of his life — a vertical or cross section, or something of that sort — instead of the entire length, breadth, and depth of it; the very grain and texture of his being. Morality is not something added to man; it is the man; and so morals is not a part of the course; it is the course. True moral teaching seeks to affect conduct indirectly by the general elevation of life. Whatever brings out the features of the soul, develops fully and harmoniously its powers and faculties, directs the aspiring self to the highest claims of manhood, frees and stimulates the ethical passion among the forces of man's nature, reveals to the individual the beauty and worth of character, and inspires the soul with a "passion for truth and righteousness that shall press towards absolute satisfaction," is moral teaching.

With this view of the question it is easy to see how instruction in morals may find a place in the course of study; or to see that it matters little if it have no place; for the teacher who tones all his work to the moral key can afford to refuse it space on the program.

If the question should yet remain, how teach a subject so as to give it moral force? the answer is, teach it; universalize it; and this universalizes the soul in its intellectual, emotional, and volitional activities. An ethical will is one that chooses universal ends, rather than special and private ones. Patriotism is the power to choose the good of the country against personal desires; and philanthropy is yet wider in its reach, embracing humanity. Nothing is more directly and effectively ethical than giving to the pupil's isolated individuality conscious relation to the universe about him; and this is done by universalizing the subject-matter with which he deals. To reach the innermost constitution of an object and find the self in it, is the true secret of organizing ethical power. One cannot touch his other self in the object, as urged under the law of method, without feeling the "ethical nudge," and being strengthened for higher activities of life.

Since man's ethical nature is not a department but the tone and attitude of his whole life, ethical training cannot be restricted to exercising the will alone. It is ethical training when the intellect is required to form accurate judgments, to bound ideas definitely, to surround facts and take their bearings, to see the other and the opposite of things, to grasp diversity of facts into unity of system.

Charity and liberality depend on training to see all sides of a question; and humility comes from a habit of being led by truth against first impressions and preconceived notions. Power of abstract thought and of complex judgment are absolutely essential to ethical action, since such power is required to adjust acts to remote and universal ends. Truth-telling requires as its basis the power to adjust the mind accurately to realities. Intellectual training is organically related to character and conduct.

In previous discussions it was frequently pointed out that every object studied has an emotional value; that an object has not been grasped in all its relations till the emotions have appropriated it. What is known as pure intellectual activity, when healthful and adequate to its object, is accompanied by a glow of feeling. If the teacher should select the Pythagorean proposition for the purpose of cultivating the intellect, in doing this very thing well, he will hear somewhere in the process a clapping of hands in the joy of demonstrative activity. In this the proposition makes its contribution to life and character. Capacity for intellectual delight is moral capacity.

Especially potent for good is the poetic elevation of spirit arising when the object is viewed as a type of ideal truth. How man is lifted over the mud-puddles of life by his power to give a poetic interpretation to common things! How dull, flat, and insipid goes life weighed down too close to the dirt, and what desperate surges of relief through dangerous indulgences! What relief when the imagination is trained to see beauty and goodness from the least suggestion of dull and customary objects! The bee carries honey away from the flower in Hawthorne's dooryard; and he thinks of throwing a benefaction on the passing breeze to sweeten the sourness and bitterness of the world. The pupil must thus be trained to see everything in its beautiful and beneficent aspect, "to sweeten the sourness and bitterness" of his after life. Such forms of thought ought to be no exceptional activity in the pupil's work; but, as so often pointed out in the course of previous discussions, it is one of the relations under which every object should be viewed. And thus in the main line of school work, and not as a side issue, all the emotional chords are attuned to beautiful harmonies, which make life rich and full and joyous — which makes for righteousness.

The problem of religion in the public school. — Like the question of morals, the difficulty is that of organizing religious instruction into the course of study; but with religion there is the more stubborn question as to whether it should have any place in the course. This may be largely a question of the use of terms. Those who claim that religion should be taught in the public school may agree with those who claim that it should not, in the sense in which they mean that it should not; and those who claim that it should not be taught may agree with those who claim that it should, in the sense in which they claim that it should.

The difficulty seems to arise in a failure to discern fundamental likenesses where differences are striking.

The church and railroads seem to have nothing in common, yet both look to the amelioration and salvation of man. Teaching a Sunday-school class and pegging shoes are not considered in the same line of activities, yet the spiritual elevation of the race is their common end. The pick and the shovel join with the sermon in eradicating sin and establishing the kingdom of heaven in the hearts of men. Education and religion must have some common, vital principle, in spite of the fact that they have been set over against each other as if they belonged to different categories, if not antagonistic. This sharp line of distinction often blinds to the best truth in both, leaving education without purity, holiness, faith, noble purpose, a striving for perfect knowledge and harmony with God — with nothing but the sharp intellect either with or without character; and religion without beauty, fullness, and vigor of life, large-minded, generous manhood — with nothing but dogma and creed and formal piety. We hear that education is a doubtful factor, having to do with the intellect, and giving reckless power unless restrained by the religious heart; that it is an affair of this world to satisfy hunger and pride, while religion is for eternity, satisfying and saving the soul.

Religion is not a branch, a department, or anything that can be added to education; but rather vitalized, purified, and quickened blood. It is the attachment and devotion of every faculty of the soul to truth, beauty, and virtue. It includes man's whole being, — his tone and temper of life, purity of heart; his striving to know and feel the true, the permanent, the eternal source of all things; his tendency of life upward toward truth and God. Whatever else you may desire to include, so much are essential elements. Neither is education a branch, a department, or anything that can be added to religion. Education is to fix the tendency of life upward; to stimulate a striving for perfection of character; to enlighten and strengthen the native tendencies of the soul; to intensify and purify, broaden and deepen, refine and enrich life by all things true, beautiful, and good; and to establish the current of being in the safe channel of spiritual activity. Education is not power unqualified, but power regulated and directed to righteous ends. The work of education is fatally defective which gives faculties power without the power of right direction; strength of life without right tendency of life. The man who is untruthful or dishonest, of mean prejudices or revengeful temper, though versed in sciences and arts, is not educated. The uncharitable, though he speak with the tongues of men and of angels, though he have the gift of prophecy, and understand all mysteries and all knowledge, lacks one element of that rounded fullness of character which is the aim of education. Though man walk up and down the dusty highways of knowledge, yet if he does not experience that self-surrender to truth, that "consciousness of living under high and beautiful laws," which destroys the last bit of egotism in him, he has missed the best education has to give. Man's attainment in departments of knowledge is something, but what he attains to in simple manhood is everything. Not ten questions of knowledge, but, ultimately, ten questions of life : —

1. Is he gentle, kind, and charitable? 2. Is he candid, simple, and without guile? 3. Is he sincere, pure, and noble? 4. Is he genial, just, and generous? 5. Is he rich and full in his inner world of experience? 6. Has he true moral self-reliance, self-restraint, self-control, self-direction? 7. Has he breadth of outlook over the physical and moral worlds? 8. Does his life flow on beautifully, joyously, towards the divine source of all things? 9. Is he delicately responsive to the music of creation? 10. Is he in harmony with the divine order of the universe?

Any statement of education in terms of mere knowledge and intellectual shrewdness, omitting the ultimate test in the spiritual tone of life — its breadth and depth; its fullness, richness, and power; its faith, hope, and aspirations; its responsive pulsations to truth, beauty, and virtue — is false in theory and unsafe in practice. In this view education must develop and strengthen whatever elements of character are essential to the highest Christian virtue.

Hence religion is already in the course; not as one of the subjects of instruction, but as a pervasive force through all subjects. If the public school cannot add religion to its course, there is nothing to prevent the teacher from spiritualizing education into religion. The fundamental tone running through the entire discussion of method is that of unity of the pupil with the spiritual, conscious life back of the phenomena of the world. In this the pupil lives and moves and has his being. The universal truth of the world's religions, present and past, is this : "We look not at the things which are seen, but at the things which are not seen : for the things which are seen are temporal; but the things which are not seen are eternal." Religion is the feeling of unity with the abiding life and spirit back of variable and vanishing phenomena. All philosophy seeks to explain this unity ; poetry idealizes it in feeling ; and education is, by systematic plan and purpose, to develop the individual into a capacity for living in conscious unity with the sustaining power of the universe. From this highest mountain peak of observation, religion and education, so sharply contrasted in the valley below, are seen as one and inseparable. When teacher and preacher rise to inspired utterance they necessarily clothe education in conception and terms of religion. Archbishop Farrar, from the side of the church, states it eloquently thus : —

"The true end of education, of whatever kind, we must set steadily before us. 'There are some who wish to know that they may know ; this is a base curiosity. There are some who wish to know that they may be known ; this is base vanity. There are some who wish to sell their knowledge ; this is base covetousness. There are some who wish to know that they may edify ; this is charity : and those who wish to be edified, and this is heavenly prudence.' The object of education is that we may learn to see and know God here and glorify Him in heaven hereafter."

Professor Laurie, from the side of the school, rises to the same level in the following : —

"Man can rise above mere world-citizenship, and become a citizen of a city not made with hands. The divine in him claims fellowship and kindred with God. He can rise to the contemplation of ideas and regard them face to face. When man attains his full stature and to communion with ideas, he raises his head above the vaporous clouds of earth and breathes an ampler ether, a diviner air. He now begins to see the cosmic order as truly a spiritual order, and returning to the ordinary life of the citizen, he descends from his Sinai not to despise the mean things of the daily life, but now rather to see the God of the mountain-top in them, and to illuminate all with a light that comes from within. He no longer sees with the eye of sense. For him nature is now bathed in that light that never was on sea or shore. The glory of setting suns, with all its splendor, is now to him only a dwelling-place for the universal spirit; the infinite variety of nature only the garment we know Him by. The palpitating thought which is all, and in all, now finds in the spirit of man a responsive pulse. It is to sow the germs of this life of the spirit that the university exists; to give food, nutrition of this kind, — to supply the spiritual manna which will never fail us in the wilderness-wandering of earthly existence, as each morning we rise to a new day."

And thus from the mountain-top the conflicts in educational thought disappear, and the complex diversity in the teaching process is seen to move in unity and harmony to the supreme good in human life.

INDEX.

"A Day in June," a reading lesson, 178.
Academic studies, 80 to 85.
Aim in teaching, 36 to 41; found in the nature of life, 42; true aim, 71.
Aims, diversity of, 36; unification of, 63.
Amazon River, as fixed, 154; as changing, 156; lesson on, 157 to 162.
Analogy between physical and spiritual life, 64; as a process of induction, 226 to 228.
A Posteriori Arguments, 240 to 245.
Application of the teaching process, 153 to 182.
Applying the General notion, 214.
A Priori Arguments, 235 to 239.
Argument, movements in, 216 to 244; the processes in, 220.
Argumentation, 184; teaching by, 219.
Argyle, Duke of, quotation from, 90.
Arithmetic, effect if knowledge of be taken away, 61; practical knowledge of, 65 to 70.
Attributes, individual, universal, 109; thinking individual through, 120; of relation, 122; of properties, 128 to 137; manner of viewing, 133 to 137.

Basis, choice of, 139; the law in choosing, 140.
Battle of Lexington, a lesson on, 169.
Beautiful, nature of, 123 to 125.
Biological sciences, rise of in the course of instruction, 243.
Boy, plural of, a lesson on, 24 to 29.
Branches in the common school, 68.

Carlyle, quotation from, 89.
Cause and effect, as attributes, 126; relation of in argumentation, 231.
Change, conception of involves purpose, 147; time, 148; cause and effect, 148; whole and part, 149; likeness and difference, 151.
Choice in life, 48.
Civilization, definition of, 57.
Class unity, 111.
Common-school, purpose of, 63; fundamental branches in, 62 to 72.

Comparison and Contrast, 143; value of, 143; laws of, 144.
Concentration, the problem of, 261.
Content, how found, 185.
Correlation of studies, the problem of, 263.
Course of study, graded, 106; formulation of, 246 to 260.

"Daybreak," a poem, as a work of art, 204.
Deduction, 216; proof in, 220.
Definition, 186; definition of, 187; steps in, 188; illustration of, 189; laws of, 191; educational value of, 192; time for making, 193.
Description, teaching by, 118.
Dewey, John W., quotation from, 183.
Difference, found in neither object, 88.
Digestion, lesson on, 168.
Diversity of aims, 36.
Division, process in exposition, 186; compared with definition, 195; steps and laws in the process, 195; educational value of, 197; moving in unity with definition, 198; illustrated by parts of speech, 199.
Drawing, reason for its study, 62.
Dynamical attributes, 130.

Education, philosophy of, v; vital question, 37; practical, 40.
Educational value of subjects, the problem of, 265.
Enriching the course of study, the problem of, 261.

"Excelsior," analysis of, 209 to 213.
Exhaustive teaching, 138.
Exposition, the process of, 184.
Extension, attribute of, 128.
Extent, how found, 185.

Factor, objective, 247; subjective, 251.
Factors in the process, 79.
Fallacies, how arise, 218; in *a priori* arguments, 237; teacher's responsibility, 239; in *a posteriori* arguments, 243; responsibility of teacher, 244.
Fallacy, law for testing, 223.
Farrar, archbishop, quotation from, 274.
Fine art, 206.
Forming the general notion, 185.
Freedom, physical, 58; spiritual, 59.
Fundamental branches, 61.

General notion, forming, 185; applying, 214.
Geography, advantages of, 62; practically taught, 65; a lesson from, 157.
Good, the nature of, 123.
Grammar, illustrations from, 189, 199.
Ground of unity, the ultimate, 93.

Harris, Dr., quotation from, 104.
Heart, a lesson on, 162.
Hickok's mental science, a quotation from, 134.
History, purpose of study, 62; a lesson from, 169.

INDEX. 279

Idea, general, how formed, 184.
Ideal truth, exposition of, 203.
Identification, 217; two phases, 226; the process of, 230.
Illustration of the teaching process, the pyramid, 11; the word boys, 24.
Individual, two ways of thinking, 116; two classes, 117; thinking through attributes, 120; by means of parts, 138; thinking one by means of another, 143; as changing, 145; an outline for thinking, 152.
Induction, 217; proof through, 225.
Instruction, course of, 246.
Interdependencies, civilized world a net-work of, 58; industrial world, 65.
Interest, the most pervasive idea, 94.

Judgment, definition of, 216.

Key to reading and literature, 207.
Knowledge, nature of, 79.

Laurie, quotation from, 275.
Law of life, the universal, 48; of teaching, 73; of unity, 97.
Laws of partition, 139 to 141.
Lesson planning, gain in, 29 to 35.
Life, aim found in nature of, 42 to 63; physical, 42; spiritual, 44; law of, 48; analogy between physical and spiritual, 64; conflicts exhibited in literature, 51; typical battles of, 53; an external process, 55.
Likeness and difference, 151.

Literature, discussion of, 204 to 214.
Longfellow, selections from, 204, 208.
Lowell, selections from, 178.

Mathematics, rise of in course of study, 247.
Matter-of-fact truth, 204.
Method, definition of, 74; a mental action, 79; universal law of, 102; two points in, 108; in definition, 188.
Morals in the public school, problem of, 267.

Narration, teaching by, 108.
Notion, general, 185.

Object, view of, guidance in teaching, 137.
Objective factor, 247.
Organic unity, 111.
Outline of thinking the individual, 152; of a pencil, 173; of the course of study, 250.

Partition, 138; law of, 139 to 143; hard to obey, 149.
Parts of speech, illustration, 199.
Pencil, an outline of, 173.
Perceptive activity, 76 to 79.
Philosophy, problem in, 79.
Physical science, rise of in course of instruction, 247.
Physiology, reason for studying, 62; illustrations from — a heart, 162; digestion, 168.
Practical subjects, 65 to 71.
Process of teaching, why two, 113.

Professional studies, 80.
Properties, primary, 128; secondary, 130.
Psychology, educational, 32.
Psychological sciences, rise of in the course of instruction, 248.
Purpose of common school, 65.
Pyramid, lesson on, 11 to 23.

Question the premise, 221; teacher's responsibility, 222.
Questions for final examination, 273.

Reading, its benefit, 67; lessons in, 176, 178, 208.
Relation, attributes of, 122; purpose and means, 122; cause and effect, 126; time and place, 127.
Relation of content to extent, 186.
Religion in the public school, problem of, 270.
Resistance, attribute of, 129.
Rousseau, quotation from, 39.

"Skipper Ireson's Ride," a reading lesson, 176.
Statical attributes, 128.
Statico-dynamical attributes, 130.
Subjects, cultural, practical, 64; in the course of instruction, 225.
Syllogism, 217; terms in, 223.

Teaching, definition of, 9; purpose of, 54; fundamental defect in, 105; by description, 118; by narration, 118; exhaustive, 138.

Teaching Process, general nature of, 1; inferences from, 4; particular nature, 5; conscious factors of, 7; organic elements of, 8; diagram of, 10; illustrations of, 12 to 24; two organic phases of, 75; two factors in, 79; specific phases, 109; as a complex whole, 246.
Thinking the individual, through its attributes, 120; by means of parts, 138; law of, 139; one individual by means of another, 143 to 145; the individual as changing, 145; the general, 183 to 245; the content of a class, 187; the extent of a class, 194.
Thorough thinking, 138.
True, nature of, 123 to 126.
Truth, practical, 104; ideal, 203.

Unity, ultimate ground of, 73; ultimate law of, 97; organic, 111; class, 111.
Universal, law, 73; attributes, 109.
University, purpose of, 65.

Value, of educational process, 19; of thinking an object systematically, 146.
Viewing attributes, manner of, 133.

Whittier, selection from, 176.
World — external, internal — how thought, 87; subjective and objective, diagram of, 103.

Zoölogy, 80.

www.ingramcontent.com/pod-product-compliance
Lightning Source LLC
Chambersburg PA
CBHW022335230426
43664CB00040B/1045